MW01641364

THE PASTORAL MINISTRY

THE PASTORAL MINISTRY

James N. McCutcheon

Abingdon
Nashville

THE PASTORAL MINISTRY

Library of Congress Cataloging in Publication Data

McCutcheon, James N., 1929-
The pastoral ministry.
1. Pastoral theology. 2. Clergy—Office. I. Title.
BV4011.M24 253'.2 78-7253

ISBN 0-687-30088-6

MANUFACTURED BY THE PARTHENON PRESS AT
NASHVILLE, TENNESSEE, UNITED STATES OF AMERICA

For my father

Chester Sample McCutcheon

(1897–1971)

He made the love of God believable;
He gave me all, in faith and wisdom,
a father can a son;
He taught me, by example, to dare
the things that count;
He was, by far, the greatest man
I've ever known.

Preface

The pastoral ministry is a science all its own. The view from inside is entirely different from that anywhere else. Nevertheless, the writing of professional books about it has increasingly been left to seminary professors and denominational officials, whose parish experience is often severely limited, out of another era or completely nonexistent.

We should not therefore be overly surprised that much advice upon which the local church minister is supposed to base everything from parish Christian education to downtown church strategy, just does not work. But to my mind, the greater tragedy is that the countless accomplishments in program design and practice, devised and currently in use by highly successful parish ministers, remain largely unpublished and unshared.

This book attempts to supply a small part of a very great lack. Its seven chapters cover the main issues of pastoral ministry, as seen by one who has spent twenty-two consecutive years attempting to practice the science. In a word, this is a book by a parish minister, for parish ministers, about the parish ministry.

As might be imagined, it is a flawed effort. Much of major importance has been only superficially touched. However, even as Gamaliel was once required to explain the entire Mosaic Law "but only for so long as he could stand on one foot," the reader is thereby spared all but the essentials. The author's evident biases may constitute an additional deficiency for some. Other competent parish ministers will surely dispute many of the findings. But this too strikes me as very much to be desired. What is urgently needed in this hour is a great deal more professional discussion among practicing parish ministers—not less. Therefore, if this little volume can act as a catalyst for a much more general reaction, it will have abundantly fulfilled its purpose.

I would not know where to begin acknowledging my indebtedness. The faculties of three great seminaries, the wisdom and kindness of two excellent senior ministers and a college chaplain under whom I apprenticed, and six or seven long cherished professional colleagues decisively influenced the outcome. The four congregations I have thus far served, by letting me learn my trade in their midst, have taught me more than either they or I shall ever know. My beloved wife, Janet, and the three children—James, Jr.; Janet, Jr.; and George—cheerfully put up with a lost summer while I was setting down what follows on paper.

But most of all I want to thank God for calling me into the parish ministry in the first place. No one loves every minute of anything. But together with the family that raised me and the other, to which I not always so successfully attempt to be an adequate husband and father, the parish ministry comprises the best of the providence God has so liberally bestowed upon me. The great German pastor Hermann Bezzel (1861–1917), almost a century ago, set down these lines which, among all that have come to my attention, best describe the thanksgivings for a calling into the pastoral ministry that well up in my heart today:

> There are greater honors and higher ranks, but there is no other office that so refreshes the weariness of the heart and brings comfort to the poor and speaks peace to the dying and shows a lost world the way home.

James Norton McCutcheon
Easter 1978
Kalamazoo, Michigan

Contents

The Parish Minister's Professional Devotional Life

Much has been made of the considerable evidence that Jesus observed a regular practice of private devotions. Commentators less frequently stress the far more important fact that these lonely spiritual exercises, as recorded in the New Testament, are always intimately related to his public ministry.[1] It is the premise of what follows that a private professional devotional life, modeled on the practice of Jesus and celebrated by monks, order priests, and parish clergy through most of the Christian centuries, remains the essential foundation of the parish ministry today.

What we shall hereafter refer to as the parish minister's professional devotional life is therefore not to be confused with family devotions, prayer groups, or even private devotions in general. The exercises described in the succeeding pages are a nontransferable personal responsibility of every parish minister. They are as important to the living out of his calling as the preparation of sermons, hospital visitation, and pastoral counseling, providing the essential standpoint, wisdom, and strength for each. And the normative model, as well as some of the principal circumstances involved in this undertaking, stand starkly revealed in this brief narrative out of the life of Jesus:

> In the morning, a great while before the day, he rose and went out to a lonely place, and there he prayed. And Simon and those

> who were with him pursued him, and they found him and said to him, "Every one is searching for you." (Mark 1:35-37)

This glimpse into Jesus' private devotional life and its parallel in Luke 4:42-43 provide at least three impressions of our Lord's habitual practice that immediately speak to the modern parish minister's professional devotional life. To begin with, our Lord invariably chose a time and a place to conduct his meditations where he was not likely to be disturbed. So these words: "a great while before the day, he rose and went out to a lonely place and there he prayed." Likewise, Jesus did not permit either those he served or even his closest professional associates (i.e., his disciples) to disturb his devotional reflections upon his public ministry. Yet finally, Jesus' professional devotional life was always threatened, and frequently terminated, by the intrusion of associates, his parish, and the needs of the world. To this point, we read that "Simon and those who were with him pursued him, and they found him and said to him, 'Every one is searching for you.'"

How many parish ministers have not, countless times, had their morning devotions ended by such real or imagined "emergencies" as they sought divine guidance and strength for the ten to sixteen hours of study, counseling, calling, and meetings that would fill to overflowing the rest of the day? Nevertheless, a proper professional devotional life remains the only sure foundation upon which an authentic parish ministry can rise. The hypocrisy and unhappiness that currently plague the parish ministry chiefly result from its absence. What many refer to as the parish minister's identity crisis derives from the same source. There can no longer be reasonable doubt that one of the chief reasons so many Christian clergymen are today leaving the parish ministry for other fields is rooted in a prior failure to establish and maintain, after the manner of Jesus and the example of earlier centuries, a serious professional devotional life.

Forbes Robinson's 1912 observations to an aspiring parish minister, on the importance of this undertaking, have never been surpassed. Several pertinent passages from his collected *Letters to His Friends* are therefore recalled here:

> One thing you must learn to do. Whatever you leave undone you must not leave this undone. Your work will be stunted and half developed unless you attend to it. You must force yourself to be alone and to pray. . . . You may be eloquent and attractive in your life, but your real effectiveness depends on your communion with the eternal world. You will easily find excuses. Work is so pressing and work is necessary. Other engagements take time. You are tired. . . . And yet. . . . the necessity is paramount, is inexorable. If you and I are ever to be of any good, if we are to be a blessing, not a curse, to those with whom we are connected, we must enter into ourselves, we must be alone with the only source of unselfishness. If we are of use to others, it will chiefly be because we are simple, pure, unselfish. If we are to be simple, pure, unselfish, it will not be by reading books or talking or working primarily, it will be by coming in continual contact with simplicity, purity, unselfishness. Heaven is the possibility of fresh acts of self-sacrifice, of a fuller life of unselfishness. You are a man and a minister in so far as you are unselfish. You cannot learn unselfishness save from the one Source. Definite habits of real devotion—these we must make and keep to and renew and increase. Then we shall gradually find that we are less dependent on self—that even in the busiest scenes we dare not act on our own responsibility—that, be the act ever so small and trifling, when we are in difficulty we shall naturally, inevitably, spontaneously turn to that place whence help alone can come.[2]

All of which leads to what, practically from the beginning, has been spoken of in the Christian church as a "rule of life."

Most of us have seen a Roman Catholic or Orthodox priest, a nun, or some religious brother sitting in a bus or walking about in a park, absorbed in a religious exercise, which they read and prayed out of a small book. These Christians were following a rule of life that in some cases had been imposed upon them by ecclesiastical authority and in others had been accepted as a voluntary religious obligation. Abbots, heads of religious orders, and bishops were the earliest publishers of these private devotional liturgies. Daily cycles of religious offices, celebrated in order houses, monastaries, and cathedrals soon proceeded from them. Until quite recently, clergy, at the time of ordination, pledged themselves to the keeping of these private devotional duties, for the benefit of both their own souls and those of their patrons or parishioners. Indeed, for sixteen centuries the principal source of spiritual support and renewal for all the church's full-time servants, as well as society's most important intercessions, was the daily round of prescribed religious exercises. Of these, the most famous, if not the most influential, was the private devotional liturgy displayed in Ignatius Loyola's (1491–1556) *Spiritual Exercises,* which became the rule of life for all Jesuit priests.

But with the Protestant Reformation and the priesthood of all believers a fundamental change occurred. Responsibility for maintaining a rule of life, formerly invested in the clergy, became the obligation of all Christians. In principle, the benefits were obvious. In fact, the results were disastrous. For the combination of placing responsibility for keeping a rule of life on all Christians, and at the same time leaving enforcement to conscience rather than to ecclesiastical authority, started a ministerial withdrawal from the keeping of any sort of rule of life that today has reached catastrophic proportions.

There is little doubt that the disappearance of the Protestant midweek service and the decline of Sunday evening public worship were preceded by a general demise in the keeping of a proper rule of life. It is equally certain that the recent popularity of Unity, speaking in tongues, various forms of pentecostalism, healing services, transcendental meditation, and prayer groups attests to a great need to fill the yawning vacuum previously occupied by widespread participation in regular private devotions.

Needless to say, the particular part of the body of Christ this defection wounds most deeply is the ordained clergy—and particularly those of that calling who are charged with the care of parish churches. For the largest number of parish ministers not only no longer pray daily for their parishioners; of even greater moment, they no longer seek divine guidance and strength for themselves. Indeed, there are few things seminaries, theological schools, and denominational bodies could do that would prove more helpful to the Christian church than to make appropriate training in the private devotional life a required element of every parish minister's formal education, as well as a prerequisite for ordination.

Twenty years of ordained service, all of them spent as a parish minister, have suggested to me four principles of procedure for keeping a proper professional rule of life by which the office may be most productively ordered:

(1) *Establish a regular time and place to observe your rule of life.* The place should be constant, as secure as possible from interruptions, and ought to offer an atmosphere conducive to professional devotions. The same standards apply to the choice of an appropriate time. No other regularly scheduled activities ought to intrude. The parish and other staff members should be asked not to bother the minister during the selected period. And the time chosen should be that most likely to support the particular purpose of the undertaking.

If only a single period for private devotions is observed, most parish ministers—and rightly so—practice their personal rule of life, after the manner of Jesus, in the very early morning. Immediately after arriving at the office or study, most of us are as alert and fresh as we shall be all day. The day's work is spread out before us. All options and possibilities are still open. The psychology of early morning is overwhelmingly that of hope, bearing intimations of new beginnings, fresh opportunity, the empty tomb, and the Resurrection. One therefore can pray for the grace, wisdom, and strength to deal with tasks yet unfaced. And most important, God and his Christ are invited into the planning and accomplishment of the day's ministry. Those parish ministers who do not observe their personal rule of life in the early morning are most likely to celebrate it in the late afternoon or evening. Here the mood is reflective. The day's ministry is almost over. Most options are already closed. The psychology of evening, peace, sleep, thanksgiving, and that "house not made with hands, eternal in the heavens," pervades everything. And God and his Christ are invited in to judge and bless what has already been done.

One of the most meaningful uses of evening devotions best occurs about the supper table and involves the entire family.

Our comings and goings, more often than not, make the evening meal the single time all of us break bread together. The psychology of evening provides not only the attitudes but the feeling for time that, in my judgment, yield the richest rewards family devotions can offer.

Always when our children were smaller, and still during Advent and Lent, we open our evening meal with one of our number reading a passage from the scriptures, another adding something from appropriate devotional literature, and a third offering prayer. During the time of prayer, there is a short period of silence, when family members can add short petitions, intercessions, or thanksgivings for matters that may be on their minds.

In any event, a brief period of evening devotions with the family is certainly a uniting and strengthening experience for all involved. But so far as a parish minister's professional devotional life is concerned, the example of Jesus remains best. If a single office is to be observed, the parish minister is well advised to locate it at the beginning rather than at the end of the working day. My own practice takes place at my office desk as soon as I arrive in my study on each working morning of the week. The exercise occupies between forty-five minutes and one hour. My parish is aware of this schedule. And except in the case of an emergency, my private devotions are not interrupted.

(2) *Devise a regular liturgy for your rule of life.* Together with the establishment of a set time and place, a regular liturgy or daily order of worship is the foundation of a parish minister's professional devotional life. One does not get very far in these matters if he or she begins by staring vacantly out into empty space and asking, What shall I do today? Parish ministers, beset with endless administrative distractions, unexpected crises, and other claims upon their attention, will soon find the keeping of a rule of life futile unless they have a clear idea of exactly what it is they are to accomplish, before the time set apart for their private devotions arrives. On this head, it is worth recalling the request of Jesus' disciples. Seeking a personal rule of life, they besought him, "Lord, teach us to pray" (Luke 11:2). To which Jesus responded not

simply with general instructions about avoiding street corners, empty phrases, and hypocrites (Matt. 6:5-7) but with a precise prescription for daily devotions—the Lord's Prayer.

A simple, logical, personally meaningful liturgy ought therefore be settled upon. The daily office, whatever its final design, should be built around the study of scripture and prayer. Beginners ought not to attempt too much. Fifteen minutes' worth of honest effort may be all one's interest span can tolerate at the outset. So be it. With faithful practice, the usable period will lengthen. Indeed, the day will all too soon arrive when the maximum amount of available time for one's professional devotional life no longer seems nearly time enough.

My rule of life opens with a brief prayer of access, or invocation, and the General Confession. This is followed by twenty minutes of Bible study, ten minutes of meditating upon nonscriptural devotional literature, and twenty minutes of private prayer (during which I reflect on yesterday's failures, seek specific help for the current day's labors, pray for such civic and parish needs as lie most heavily on my heart, intercede individually for each person on my parish prayer list, and pray for each individual in my own family). I conclude by reciting the General Thanksgiving, the Apostle's Creed, and the Lord's Prayer. It has been my habit to pay close attention to the church year in the selection of readings and prayers. This imparts a refreshing variety to the exercise, as well as immersing my little part of the Kingdom work in the infinitely larger and strengthening life of the whole Christian church. Like many other past and present parish ministers, I have discovered that what happens in the first hour of my working day is alone what makes all the rest possible.

(3) *Make immediate relevance to past and future parish ministry the focus of your rule of life.* For the active parish minister, more than most other Christians, a vital personal devotional life needs to concentrate upon that which is immediate and present. As worthy as it may be to pray for the day when "all nations shall beat their swords into plowshares" or for "the second coming of Christ," it is far more important to pray for the parishioner who, at that hour, lies in the

hospital with a broken hip, the troubled marriage you will counsel later in the morning, the grief-stricken widow whose husband is to be buried tomorrow, or even your own child's flagging efforts to master third-year French. These familiar words of Jesus speak with special force to the question of where the parish minister's daily rule of life ought to be focused: "Therefore, do not be anxious about tomorrow, for tomorrow will be anxious for itself. Let the day's own trouble be sufficient for the day" (Matt. 6:34). For finally, nothing more quickly snuffs out a clergyman's professional devotional life than a half hour of turgid cant over what is vague, abstract, mainly God's business, or somebody else's problem altogether.

My own practice takes on its greatest vitality as I work, one by one, through the names on my parish prayer list. This ever-changing roster includes those in the hospital, our homebound members, individuals I am counseling, parishioners known to be struggling with problems, the bereaved, the members of my church staff, each member of my personal family, and a diverse collection of others for whom, as the old prayer has it, I feel particularly "bound to pray," After two decades of such supplications, I still am awed at the results. Time and countless time again, the few seconds spent praying for a particular person has enabled me to accomplish a ministry, later in that same day, of which I had despaired. Likewise, seemingly insoluble misunderstandings and hostilities have miraculously vanished through, I am persuaded, the effect of "ceaseless prayer." Indeed, any mature parish minister knows he accomplishes little by human strength alone. But if one will keep and seriously pray over a personal parish prayer list each day, he or she will not be long in discovering that marvelous divine assistance of which the apostle writes: "I know how to be abased, and I know how to abound. . . . I can do all things in him who strengthens me" (Phil. 4:12-13).

(4) *Keep to your personal rule of life despite changing attitudes.* Nothing is more fickle than our feelings. Ups and downs alternate constantly. The result is a very powerful

tendency to conduct private devotions only when one feels like it. This is a tragic mistake for anyone. It is a fatal mistake for the parish minister. For if we seek God's presence and the Lordship of Christ only when we feel good, divine guidance and strength are unlikely to reach those moments in our parish ministry which require them most. If we seek God's presence and the Lordship of Christ only when things go so badly we can no longer manage alone, then a "foxhole" devotional mentality develops, and we are unlikely to offer God due thanksgivings and praise. Neglect of either the times of good feeling or the times of bad feeling is therefore equally crippling to the parish minister's professional devotional life. Again here, we may learn much from the example of Jesus. Part of the strength of our Lord's private devotional life derives from the fact it was weatherproof. Nowhere does this characteristic stand forth more clearly than in the return of the seventy, where we find Jesus counseling three score and ten of the church's very first ministers that they ought not to make too much of either their successes or failures, but rather they ought to concentrate on thanking God that their "names are written in heaven" (Luke 10:20).

If the parish minister is to grow in value and effectiveness and eventually just to survive, his or her rule of life needs therefore to become a habit. It must be pursued with the same faithfulness we apply to sleeping every night and eating three times a day. But there is another and even greater reason that these daily exercises must not be done or left undone according to personal whim. Stated simply, our ordination and the derived responsibility for the "cure of souls" require such regular devotional work of us. The parish ministry is but an extension of God's answer to our prayers. Sermons are expositions of God's Word only when the preacher begins their preparation by prayerfully inquiring what is to be made of a particular text, in the hearing of a particular congregation, on this or that particular Sunday. Pastoral ministry is God's healing and the cure of souls only if divine Grace, not simply human ingenuity, constitutes the therapy. But finally, faithfully keeping a daily rule of life is an inescapable duty for any who acknowledge a serious calling of Christ to "Feed my lambs . . . Tend my sheep . . . Feed my sheep" (John 21:15-19). Every parish church is filled with despairing, misguided, error-prone, sinful Christians who pray for neither themselves nor anything else. So, from the beginning, it has been a particular duty of parish ministers to pray for each distressed member of their flocks. That is precisely what the "elders" (one of several first-century titles for the parish minister) are commanded to do in this familiar instruction:

> Let them pray over [the needy], . . . and the prayer of faith will save the sick man, and the Lord will raise him up; and if he has committed sins, he will be forgiven. . . . The prayer of a righteous man has great power in its effects" (James 5:14-16).

The particular virtues of the morning office and the evening office have already been discussed. Occasional offices now need to be considered. These are of paramount importance in their own right, and in addition actually bind the other two together.

The three most common occasional offices are the parish minister's private devotional observances in connection with calling at hospitals or on the homebound, pertaining to sermons, and in the context of crisis counseling. Once more, the example of Jesus is normative. Again and again, in the very midst of his pastoral ministry, we find our Lord reaching to God in private prayer. Invariably the communion is brief. Always it is focused upon the ministry at hand. Wherever possible, the private devotional effort precedes the particular ministry, although not infrequently a brief thanksgiving follows its accomplishment.

A familiar example of his practice may be discoverd in the raising of Lazarus. After ordering that the stone be removed from the mouth of the tomb, "Jesus lifted up his eyes and said, 'Father, I thank thee that thou has heard me. I knew that thou hearest me always . . . ' " (John 11:41-42). The lesson to be drawn from this incident is essential to an effective parish ministry. In a word, parish clergy ought habitually to reach out for God and his Christ prior to undertaking significant professional duties. Then the sickroom, the crisis counseling, the sermon, or the church meeting may be faced in the strength of the Lord, with assurance that divine assistance will support the ministry and shape its outcome. Indeed, when such succor is not sought, the minister goes forth in his or her own strength alone; such prayers and counsel as may be offered are but hollow efforts to impress a human audience; and the end of everything is another minister undone, in spirit if not in fact, by the hypocrisy of what he or she is about.

Two stories out of my own past may serve to illustrate both the good and bad practice of occasional offices. Very early in my first pastorate, I was called to a local hospital late at night. Getting out of my car in a snow-filled hospital parking lot, I noticed the dean of the local clergy, a saintly minister of his early eighties sitting some distance off in his parked automobile. Thinking he might be ill, I went over and asked if he was all right. "I am fine," he said. And then almost as an afterthought, he added: "I am praying, as is my habit, that Jesus will go with me into this hospital tonight. For nothing we preachers ever do in hospitals is worth doing when he doesn't." Since that long ago evening, my friend's practice has also been mine.

The other event occurred a few years ago. While on vacation, my wife and I attended Sunday morning worship at a church boasting a famous preacher, which was filled well beyond its seven-hundred-seat capacity. At the appointed time, the great man arose to preach. He intoned that lovely petition from the psalter: "Let the words of my mouth and the meditation of my heart be acceptable in thy sight, O Lord, my rock and my redeemer" (Ps. 19:14). And then he proceeded to deliver as his own, with considerable feeling and an abundance of oratorical gestures, one of Halford Luccock's sermons.

I came away from the latter experience wondering that a man so far advanced in the parish ministry could nevertheless be such a hypocrite in the things of God. The plagiarism was deplorable. But what that sermon revealed about the clergyman who delivered it was tragic. For behind that polished mouthing of another man's sermon lived a hollow parish minister, feeding as did those ancient Pharisees on the dead husks of hypocrisy (Matt. 23:1-6), who simply could not have had a meaningful professional devotional life of his own.

I shall conclude these observations on the parish minister's proper spiritual exercises with a final citation from the writings of one who truly took Jesus' personal practice as his model, and therefrom derived a daily rule of life that any cleric might envy. In 1937, Georges Bernanos published *The Diary of a Country Priest.* These few sentences from that work reveal, more than most volumes, exactly how the parish minister's keeping of a proper professional rule of life feels—as well as what it can mean to oneself, one's parish, Christ, and God:

> This morning I prayed hard for my parish, my poor parish, my first and perhaps my last, since I ask no better than to die here. My parish! The words can't even be spoken without a kind of soaring love. . . . I know that my parish is a reality . . . it is not a mere administrative fiction, but a living call of the everlasting church. But if only the good God would open my eyes and unseal my ears, so that I might behold the face of my parish and hear its voice. Probably that is asking too much. The face of my parish! The look in the eyes. . . . They must be gentle, suffering, patient eyes. I feel they must be rather like mine when I cease struggling and let myself be borne along in the great invisible flux that sweeps us all helter-skelter, the living and the dead, into the deep waters of Eternity. And those would be the eyes of all Christianity, of all parishes—perhaps of the poor human race itself. Our Lord saw them from the cross. "Forgive them for they know not what they do."[3]

Goal Setting, Staffing, and Administration

Most congregations have not recently thought about why they exist. At the time of a pastoral change, many denominations urge, if not insist, that the parish leadership team prepare a "local church profile" for the benefit of clergy who might be interested in assuming the pastorate. But these instruments, more often than not, only testify to the existing confusion. Filled with ecclesiastical platitudes and noble fantasies, the largest number project a disabling lack of self-understanding as to why their particular community of faith gathers where it does, and what constitutes its particular Christian mission. What invariably does come through clearly is that the church looks to its next pastoral settlement to provide the minister who will solve all its problems. Which is to say, it expects to secure a minister with the professional skills of Harry Emerson Fosdick and the administrative talent of the president of General Motors—one who is also able to walk on water.

Few of us possess even a modicum of these talents. Hence, exaggerated expectations are cause for alarm. But the deficiencies were there before the new minister was called and are not of his or her devising. Therefore, assuming the congregation can be induced to work through to a clear understanding of where it is and where it ought to be going, these worries can be transmuted into opportunities.

The means to accomplishing this end lie in goal setting, proper staffing, and a viable administrative process. How the parish minister best applies his or her energies to these tasks will occupy the remainder of this chapter.

The earliest Christian communities produced a definition of what every Christian parish church properly is, that has never been bettered. Paul, original architect of parochial Christianity as well as of the church's world mission, was its author. The apostle viewed every parish church in Christendom as a foreign embassy of the Kingdom of heaven, all its individual members as foreign ambassadors, and the sole purpose for the existence of both as being to transact the Kingdom of heaven's business in a hostile and foreign land. Thus these familiar words, which the majority of Christian congregations have always either chosen to ignore or never understood:

> From now on, therefore, we regard no one from a human point of view; even though we once regarded Christ from a human point of view, we regard him thus no longer. Therefore if any one is in Christ, he is a new creation; the old has passed away, behold, the new has come. All this is from God, who through Christ reconciled us to himself and gave us the ministry of reconciliation. . . . So we are ambassadors for Christ, God making his appeal through us. . . . For . . . our commonwealth is in heaven, and from it we await a Savior, the Lord Jesus Christ, who will change our lowly body to be like his glorious body, by the power which enables him even to subject all things to himself. (II Cor. 5:16-20; Phil. 3:18-21)

The aptness of this definition to our present situation is overwhelming. Even were it not the biblical blueprint for the local Christian community, the self-confidence, power, and integrity released, in any body of Christians who establish this model as the shape and substance of their congregation, will prove nothing short of miraculous. Now we are no longer a dying downtown church at the end of a long-dead trolley car line, or a noncompetitive brick functional church that has already lost the good fight to network television, the golf links, and a variety of water sports. No! Now we are an outpost of the Kingdom of heaven, one of many thousands of foreign embassies in America, all spliced together by "one Lord, one faith, one baptism, one God and Father of us all" (Eph. 4:5). And our business is neither our own nor our nation's. We are a local community of faith, a parish church, only because the Kingdom of heaven, whose rulers are God and his Christ, established us, as one of its foreign embassies, on the corner of West Main and Park Avenue. Our continuance there depends upon decisions and circumstances by no means entirely of our own devising. But while we are there, with sufficient Christians and resources to do something, it is God's agenda that must be discovered and his mission that must be accomplished.

There is nothing more important in this hour than for the parish churches of America to understand what they really are in God's sight. If all accomplished this by first light tomorrow, they would change the face of America by nightfall. But even though such dreams are about as likely of fulfillment as our forebears' hopes of "converting the world to Christ in one generation," any parish with the will to do so can become a true foreign embassy of the Kingdom of heaven. And in that action, it will have taken the most important step toward setting truly Christian parish goals. Let us now examine the practicalities of such an endeavor.

Beginning with the minister, the parish must approach the goal-setting task theologically. Too many churches operate on a survival mentality alone, imagining that so many new members, brought in on any terms, and a budget of such a size, raised by promoting "a program that will sell," constitute the most sensible parish goals. One large church, located a short distance away, still regularly approaches new member prospects with assurances that "membership in our parish will be good for your business." Some years ago, another venerable church, in a different city, attempted to increase its membership by guaranteeing all prospective communicants that "it is our church's policy never to take collective stands on controversial social issues." These, of course, are extreme examples of the bad fruit that invariably proceeds from misunderstanding what parish chuches are in God's sight, and hence improper goal setting. Parish churches never thrive on these terms for very long. What parish ministers therefore need most to help their people understand is that all truly Christian priorities are anwers to the question, What do God and his Christ desire us to do for the Kingdom of heaven, today and tomorrow, here in this place?

Once this idea has been strongly implanted and generally accepted, the parish minister should urge upon the governing bodies of the church the calling of a congregational meeting to elect a long-range planning committee. This organization should represent, as fully as possible, all boards, committees, age groups, and factions, and should be charged with studying the present and future situation of the church, with the intention of presenting to the congregation possible answers to the question posed in the last sentence of the preceding paragraph.

The goal-setting process is now institutionally structured and can begin. The church properties are as good a place as any to start. Where are our parish house and sanctuary located? What needs of the immediately surrounding community might they serve? In the answers to these queries lie important hints as to whether the congregation ought to stay where it is, merge, or relocate.

An examination of present and potential "inreach" and "outreach" naturally follows. Taken together, the data gathered here will begin to outline the shape of a truly Christian local mission. The inreach survey ought to be initiated by an audit of the church rolls; a projection of probable membership patterns for the future; an evaluation of the worship, educational, and pastoral needs of the current and anticipated congregation; and a careful study of the parish by-laws, with an eye to determining whether or not they will enable or hinder the coming Christian mission. The outreach survey should be based on direct interviews with major civic leaders and leading social service agencies, together with letters of inquiry to all significant community institutions, requesting information or proposals as to how the congregation, through its properties and resources, might prove most useful to the community. From these data, proposals for a substantial local Christian outreach mission will soon materialize.

Next the long-range planning committee should report to the congregation. No subordinate body should pass judgment on its findings and proposals; for unless each member of the congregation is given ample opportunity to discuss, amend, and finally own the long-range planning committee's report, general support will not be forthcoming. Sufficient time, therefore, must be allowed for the long range planning committee's report to percolate through the entire congregation. A comprehensive written analysis of significant findings and proposals should be published to the membership. Then a number of open meetings should be held at which any or all parts of the report can be questioned, criticized, amended, or discarded. My suggestion is that final action on the report be taken at a formal meeting—if convenient, the annual business meeting—of the parish. As presented on that occasion, the report of the long-range planning committee will usually contain specific parish goals and proposals for action. Sometimes, however, especially where widespread distrust or a serious parish controversy lies in the immediate background, it is better to move more slowly. Then only the long-range planning committee's findings will be dealt with, and the setting of specific parish goals and the adoption of action proposals will wait upon further work by the long-range planning committee and a subsequent meeting of the congregation.

What are some examples of parish goals? Depending upon the local congregation's unique needs and opportunities, the parish goals might include any or a combination of building programs, by-laws revision, development of local civic uses of the church program, a new parish Christian education program, public worship redesign, increasing the congregation's monetary contributions to the wider mission of the church, or outreach evangelism. Since the resources of all congregations are limited (and particularly its capacity for assimilating major changes), the energies and funds of the congregation need to be carefully applied. Designated parish goals must be set, with a clear congregational understanding of what will be accomplished at the outset and which projects will necessarily be deferred until later. Most congregations are capable of working toward more than one parish goal at a time. Where possible, it is an excellent idea to do so, since more church members, each with definite personal priorities, will feel that at least some of the things they believe to be of primary importance are getting done.

It is also an excellent idea to be working concurrently on projects that have to do with the local Christian mission, both as inreach and outreach. In this fashion, the two major congregational biases are both served, and neither one's own constituents nor the neighbors' needs are ignored. However, when hard choices must be made, providing the congregation has previously come to a legitimate conviction that God wants them to continue as a foreign embassy of the Kingdom of heaven where they are, the priorities served first should be those which will ensure the local community's vitality. Some congregations have stayed in barren places until they died, because their buildings were historical monuments. Others, who should have stayed where they were, and did, expired unnecessarily because they spent themselves on outreach without paying responsible attention to those necessities of inreach, which would have permitted them to remain vigorous communities of faith. Challenging parish goals, which meet both the congregation's parochial needs and those of the area in which the church building is located, are the best guarantee of any parish church's continued Christian usefulness.

From parish goals and priorities, the parish program emerges. And when the things the local congregation will attempt to accomplish over the next three, five, and ten years are laid out, the parish leadership team and the senior minister can begin putting together a staff sufficient to accomplish them.

Of course, parish life goes on while the goal setting is in progress. Hence some staff will already be employed before directions and priorities are fully understood. However, any local church is well advised, while goal setting is in process, to leave its staff options open as long as it can, even if this means struggling for a while with a partial staff. When new pastorates are established, senior ministers all too frequently fill the positions in their predecessor's administration, or recruit some equally abstract staff of personal devising—and only afterward raise the question of what each staff member is to do. Obviously, to the extent it is humanly possible, new staff members should be recruited only to fill completely worked-out positions, which fit into a developed process of implementing parish priorities and goals. Many churches today hire interim help until their goal-setting process is accomplished, in order to avoid commitments to permanent staff members with skills and interests they very shortly will not need. This is an excellent strategy, especially for congregations engrossed in the establishment of a new pastorate or in a major restudy program.

In any event, and under all circumstances, the success or failure of a local church is greatly influenced by the quality of its staff. Unlike even a moderately sized business, a local church offers no hiding places for marginal performers. Each member of a church staff is always out front, and what he or she does or does not accomplish will fundamentaly affect the church as a whole. Therefore, given the crucial importance of staff, the remainder of this chapter will be devoted to two interrelated matters upon which the personnel issue in the local church finally turns—staff options and staff administration.

Staff Options

Let us begin with ordained clergy. The guiding principle in the hiring of clergy is that only a sufficient number should be employed to cover authentic ministerial functions. A great many of America's wealthier churches hire more than are required. By so doing, ordained clergy end up working at tasks lay specialists or volunteers could do better; much money is wasted; staff bickering develops because underemployed ministers are constantly getting in one another's way; and, as a result, both the image and the profession of the parish ministry are diminished.

The most important staff position in any parish church is

that of the senior minister. The fortunes of pastorates ultimately turn on whether or not productive mutuality exists between the minister who occupies this office and the congregation he or she serves. Therefore, initial attention needs to be given to this subject.

In keeping with the purpose of this book as a resource for parish ministers, the business of securing a pastoral settlement will be viewed solely from the senior minister's standpoint. Nevertheless, the same principles apply to clergy seeking subordinate positions on multiple staffs as well. However, one thing needs to be made clear at the outset. What follows is by no means adequate to the manifold challenges involved in securing a pastorate. Any minister actively engaged in this venture is urged to begin by carefully reading some comprehensive study of the subject, such as Robert G. Kemper's excellent *Beginning a New Pastorate.*[1]

As to the general shape of the undertaking, each communion within the American church has its own unique processes and procedures for affecting pastoral settlements. Essential to most of these systems are a dossier (which the individual discussed has certain major responsibilities for completing) and a formal method for putting parish ministers seeking a pastorate, and parish churches seeking a minister, in touch with each other.

Concerning the dossier, complete candor is always the best policy. Any of us can find half a dozen friends willing to supply us with extravagant references, and much of what we write about ourselves in the autobiographical sections will never be checked. But what is gained by misrepresentation? Before the first year of a new pastorate is out, the congregation knows exactly what we can and cannot do, what we do or do not believe, and therefore whether or not it has made a mistake. Indeed, the beginning of more unhappy pastorates than no one but God will ever know, is a congregation that imagined it was getting one sort of a minister, only to find itself afflicted with quite another.

But the candor coin has two sides. The materials handed out by parish churches seeking a minister are just as liable to be largely fiction. Often they overstate membership figures and fail to report major controversies, while the circumstances surrounding the last minister's mysterious departure and the most recent half dozen disastrous every-member canvasses are nowhere mentioned. That is why interested candidates should request a current membership audit (together with an age breakdown of those reported), an accounting as to the number of current pledging units (with a categorized dollar-per-week breakdown), and the names and addresses of the parish's last three ministers (together with the privilege of communicating with them).

If, after all this, negotiations turn serious, four specific issues should be thoroughly checked out before one ought to allow his or her name to go before the congregation of a parish church as the pastoral committee's candidate:

1. The prospective minister should request and study the parish church's by-laws to make certain he or she understands fully the office and duties as described therein. Of critical importance are those by-law articles which define the minister's role as staff administrator. More on this subject will be offered later in the chapter. For the moment, it will be sufficient to observe that, unless or until all formal by-law conditions of employment are agreeable, any proffered call should be refused.

2. The contractual arrangements must be complete, equitable, and in writing. Particular attention ought to be given to the frequency of salary review, the fringe benefits offered, whether the congregation is committed to cost-of-living increments, and what sort of a parsonage or housing allowance is to be provided. The importance of these matters to the family life of the minister will be discussed in the final chapter of this book. For the moment, since the topic is goal setting, staffing, and administration, let us concentrate on the effect of the minister's contract on staff quality and morale.

Wherever the senior minister is victimized by an inadequate contract, subordinate staff will be even more shabbily treated. Such pastorates therefore open in double jeopardy. It soon becomes impossible either to hire or to keep good staff. Morale becomes a permanent problem. And the stingy parish may be counted upon to lay all the resulting unhappiness on the parsonage doorstep of the senior minister. No minister should ever accept the intolerable burdens imposed by an inequitable contract—or the call of any congregation that offers one.

3. The prospective minister should seek a detailed explanation of what the congregation sees itself wanting to accomplish over the next ten years. Candidates can do pastoral committees a world of good by assisting them in thinking through their prospects and goals. In the process, it will become clear whether the minister's particular talents and interests match those which the parish's hopes will require. There are times a minister may accept a call where the match-up of talent and interest is considerably less than exact. But that should only occur if the prospective minister has firm grounds for believing the parish's goals are deficient, and is confident of his or her own ability to lead the congregation into better purposes. Frequently a congregation is fundamentally divided respecting future directions. The wise minister will not accept a call until a solution, suitable to all major factions, has been worked out. Finally, and in any event, if the job described and the gifts and interests of a particular minister differ in significant ways, a call should never be accepted, no matter what other attractions or mutualities may exist.

4. No minister should ever accept a call to a parish (either as senior or associate minister) who has not, after much prayer, been convinced that he or she has an election to that office from God. Of course, long before any call is offered, serious prayer should have begun. If one leaves the final decision to God, innumerable unnecessary pains and pressures disappear. Not being offered a call to a desired parish is infinitely less disappointing when God is clearly understood to be chairman of the only pastoral committee that really matters. Likewise, when a call is offered by a congregation to which a minister feels unmistakably drawn, he or she can then venture into what is always God's great unknown with that peerless yet pride-free confidence of which Isaiah spoke: "I am honored in the eyes of the Lord, and my God has become my strength" (Isa. 49:5).

Now let us turn to the associate minister. Within the

ordained ranks, a number of distinct categories exist. Among full-time active clergy, the two largest groups are apprentice associate ministers and professional associate ministers. The first group comprises recent seminary graduates who join a multiple staff in order to gain experience as preparation for assuming a pastorate of their own. These men and women usually remain with the parish for a period of two to four years. Budget-conscious congregations are often attracted to them because they may be hired for considerably less than an experienced professional associate minister. The disadvantages of an apprentice associate minister are that the senior minister must give considerable attention to the associate's training. About the time these young ministers start becoming really useful to the parish, they are attracted away into churches of their own; and the parish is impelled to invest time, effort, and money in seeking still other associate ministers at distressingly frequent intervals.

The chief advantage of apprentice associate ministers to the parish church is their attractiveness to young people. As shall be urged in a later chapter, it is an excellent practice to assign an enthusiastic young minister to the parish youth fellowships and its confirmation class. Most ministers over thirty, male or female, do not have the rapport with or interest in adolescents that younger colleagues do. Unfortunately, a minority of just-ordained clergy consider youth work demeaning or simply something to be suffered. The parish that hands its young people over to this kind of an individual has hired a problem, and the sooner the associate takes up some other sort of ministry elsewhere, the better it will be for all concerned.

Professional associate ministers are clergy who have made a career decision, temporary or permanent, to work in a parish church for which another ordained minister has overall responsibility. The great majority of these men and women are gifted professionals, capable of providing superior performance in many if not all aspects of ministry. Most have elected to be professional associate ministers in order to concentrate their gifts in a particular area of service. Others do not care for the "generalist" role required of a senior minister, or for the administrative responsibilities that position involves.

But whatever the reasons and however he or she came to this calling, a good professional associate minister in a multiple-staff situation is a treasure beyond price. Consider these factors. An ordained minister with five to forty years' experience in parish ministry does not require basic training and brings immediate expertise to the program and pastoral ministry. He or she usually plans on staying for an indefinite period of time and does not regard the associate minister's role as, in any sense, a temporary stop on the way to professional maturity. In particular, professional associate ministers customarily offer a much stronger parish ministry to present and prospective members than do apprentice associates; and as a group, they are inclined to be far more amenable than apprentice associates to undertaking home calling and new-member recruitment.

Therefore, parish churches and senior ministers who desire to emphasize youth programming are generally well advised to seek an apprentice associate minister; while those wishing to stress parish calling, new-member recruitment, and long-term program development will do better by employing a professional associate. The distinctions discussed above are recognized by the fact that parishes large enough to employ three clergy commonly seek, in addition to a senior minister, one apprentice and one professional associate minister.

The growing number of retired clergy offers still another excellent source of professional staff. In recent years, improved retirement programs have allowed scores of excellent parish ministers to leave full-time Christian service at sixty-five. These dedicated professionals often desire to remain in the parish ministry on a part-time basis. Their vast experience and minimal income needs make them ideal additions to any parish staff. In years past, I have received support in parish ministry, of a quality unavailable from any other source, through the efforts of two outstanding retired ministers who accepted positions as ministers to the parish.

And we cannot forget the women! Most seminaries are now

graduating more women than ever before who hope to establish life careers in parish ministry. It is to be hoped that significant numbers of them will soon be entering pastorates of their own, and that the American church will thereby truly become an equal-opportunity employer. That goal can be substantially advanced if more churches begin calling just-graduated women clergy as apprentice associates. Those who have one already know that a woman minister brings values to the local congregation's mission and life that no male minister can hope to provide.

Then there are lay employees. Parish churches have always hired lay people as custodians, secretaries, bookkeepers, and musicians. Only lately have many come to realize their desirability as staff members for the congregation's program as well.

An attractive young matron, with children in school and time on her hands, makes an excellent parish visitor who can free up hours of the ordained clergy's working day. A public-school teacher, retired to her kitchen and washtubs by family responsibilities, will frequently jump at the chance to become some church's director of Christian education. Jobs such as these are invariably part time and ought to be developed on narrow job descriptions. The key to success is employing committed Christians possessing skills or professional training in the specific task assigned.

Hiring part-time staff members from among church members needs to be approached with extreme caution. If a parish member is installed in a salaried position, other parishioners who wanted the job may be offended. Volunteers sometimes resent working on tasks for which another church member is being paid. And church members who join the part-time salaried staff of their parish church do not always manage to maintain proper distinctions between their work obligations and their privileges as parishioners.

The one other comment that ought to be made about staffing options concerns the desirability, where possible, of becoming a staff member's "second employer." With inflation annually outstripping member pledge increases, not having to provide the major income and full fringe-benefit package for a staff member (who may also be the sole support of a family) marvelously relieves the church budget. Full-time positions ought to exist only to cover full-time jobs. Clergy, custodians, and secretaries, in most parishes, will necessarily be full-time employees. Music directors, Christian educators, program implementers, parish callers, and organists often need not be. The other principal advantage of part-time employees, besides those advantages related to the budget, is the opportunity for the church to acquire the benefits of a greater variety of specific skills through employing a number of uniquely talented individuals on narrow job descriptions, rather than one or two full-time generalists who must cover a range of duties that may extend considerably beyond both their training and their interests.

Twenty years ago, most multiple staffs were peopled by a handful of full-time generalists. My present staff has only four full-time employees, two of them are clergy, one a secretary, and the other a custodian. The six remaining staff members are lay specialists working on narrow job descriptions on a part-time basis. We are the second employer of three, and in no case the primary employer of the principal breadwinner of a family. Wages and other benefits, for all positions, rank with the best offered elsewhere for similar work. Our parish program is considerably richer and more varied because of the diversity of talent. And today we spend a substantially smaller proportion of our church budget on maintaining staff than was the case with most churches of our size just a decade ago.

The opportunities and economies described above are not—be it known—limited to large chuches. Small churches with modest budgets, by following these suggestions, can reap equally satisfying benefits. But assuming that the previously discussed goal setting is undertaken, the most singular advantage of employing part-time lay specialists on narrow job descriptions for work where an ordained minister or full-time worker is not needed, still is to be discovered in the staff flexibility thus provided, and the constant opportunity for bringing new and particular skills to bear on ever-changing parish priorities.

Staff Administration

Having a good staff is the beginning. But adequate staff administration is the key to achieving staff performance commensurate with the abilities of those hired. Indeed, the more competent the personnel on a parish church staff, the more bad administration will be resented. Competent Christians, employed in skilled or professional capacities, usually are strongly motivated to get a job done. Unnecessary confusion, ambiguous goals, and indecisive leadership always produce frustration. More than one excellent church staff has come to grief because the low state of administration kept everyone constantly off balance, in one another's hair, and devoid of any collective purpose.

The senior minister, be he or she the only cleric or one of twelve, is the person responsible for administrating the staff. Even if the church by-laws and working policies do not say so, it behooves that individual not to be under any illusions respecting things as they actually are. He or she may not get credit for successes, but the senior minister will absolutely be called on the carpet for staff failures. Therefore, as Wallace Robbins, former president of Meadville Seminary and long-time professor of pastoral sciences at the University of Chicago, used to tell his students: "Any minister is a fool to demand more authority than his responsibilities require. But he's an even bigger fool if he doesn't insist upon at least that much."

Just so! Too much concern has long been lavished on the possibility that the senior minister will use his or her administrative prerogatives to tyrannize the staff. The real problem lies in exactly the opposite direction. The senior minister is under orders, from both God and the parish, all the time. A plethora of church organizations and officers exist to control administrative autocrats and staff abusers. But who protects the senior minister from the parish that either will not or does not understand the imperative necessity of supplying its chief administrator with the authority requisite to do the job assigned?

The following arrangements constitute the minimal conditions required for the senior minister to function effectively as staff administrator: (1) The parish by-laws should indicate that the senior minister bears administrative responsibility for staff performance; (2) the senior minister should have veto power over all staff appointments; (3) subordinate staff, both clergy and lay, must have the senior minister's administrative authority spelled out in pre-employment interviews and in formal employment contracts; (4) working policies and job descriptions, completely elaborating the administrative structure, need to be worked up and adopted for all staff members; and (5) the senior minister should report at least annually to the parish personnel committee on each staff member's performance, besides immediately consulting with that body when any serious personnel problem arises. The personnel committee should also, incidentally, be available to any other member of the staff for the confidential airing of complaints or suggestions. But the personnel committee must keep clear as to its primary function—to protect and facilitate the parish church's administrative structure and process.

Twenty years of experience in multiple-staff churches, both as apprentice associate and as senior minister, have convinced me that all concerned are happiest when the lines of authority are clear and the senior minister is unquestionably the administrative head of the staff. Except in those few cases where tyrannical senior ministers held sway, staff members who are not adequately fulfilling their responsibilities have always made up the majority of those who objected to the senior minister's prerogatives as staff administrator. Staff members who are doing their jobs well tend to appreciate a strong administrator. For such a senior minister sees that colleagues receive due credit for accomplishments, that all have full range and resources to exploit their talents, and that minor parish complaints are kept off staff members' backs.

As to the job itself, until you have tried it, no one can tell another what a thankless and demanding job staff administration in a parish church actually is. Many a minister with a part-time custodian, a volunteer secretary, and the local piano teacher as choir director has looked with envy at his professional neighbor who possesses a staff of eight or ten and leads a large church just down the street. But all the senior ministers I have ever known in the latter situation have many times wished they had only themselves to worry about—and even that they might go back to the simple life of their first parish again.

So much for the administrator. Something now needs to be said about the daily details of staff administration.

One of the two or three most important reasons a senior minister ought to operate out of an office at the church is so that he or she can be constantly available to the church staff. You can not administrate if you are not around. When a staff member needs a consultation or a decision, most often it is wanted right then. Delay impedes progress and frustrates. Staff members whose boss does not keep regular office hours soon are emulating the senior minister's example. Beyond that, not keeping regular office hours at the church has similar ill effects on parishioners. Members of the leadership team, usually busy people themselves, do not appreciate constantly being told: "I'm sorry the minister isn't here at the moment. He will return your telephone call later." Not infrequently, consistent absence fuels a general suspicion that, much of the time, the senior minister is not on the job at all. And that is a situation where the appearance is as disastrous as the fact!

A weekly staff meeting, however, remains the most important single event in effective staff administration. It is wise to hold these meetings as early as possible, on the first regular staff working day of the week. My practice of taking Mondays off places our weekly staff meeting at 9:30 A.M. on Tuesdays. We bring in a lay volunteer to cover the telephones, and the entire program and office staff sits down by itself for a meeting that rarely lasts less then an hour and a half. We open with prayer. Then the week's events are surveyed. I go completely through my schedule. Each staff member, in turn, does the same. Schedule conflicts, program problems, and departmental plans are explained and discussed. Then we turn to general issues—possibly a look at major events over the next month, a particular staff member's problems with a program, or the longer-range goals we are committed to accomplishing.

In all this discussion, a single principle dominates. Within goals, guidelines, and policies established by the congregation or its representative boards and committees, we, as a church staff, strive to function as a mutually supportive team of professionals and friends. Our aim is to arrive at consensus decisions. That is to say, no staff member gets run over. All opinions are heard and considered. We will continue a discussion of some program or policy issue until either we have produced a collective determination acceptable to all staff members, or until it is clear that a stalemate has been reached. Only in the last circumstance (and stalemates probably occur in something less than 5 percent of all staff decisions) do I, as the senior minister, make the final determination. This is an action that I always take with regret, only out of necessity, and ever in the knowledge that the buck stops here.

Effective measures for criticizing or correcting staff performance are also imperative. The senior minister should always discuss any but flagrant problems in private with the staff member concerned. If confidentiality is respected, most staff shortcomings or personality conflicts can be resolved by a private consultation in the senior minister's office, to which no one but the two are privy. If, however, substantial anger, serious misrepresentations, blatant insubordination, or a major moral violation is involved, the senior minister ought to have at least two members of the personnel committee or other officers of the church present when subsequent consultations occur.

But the first rule is that administrative correction or criticism ought to proceed by due process through carefully escalating stages in which the senior minister's aim is to resolve the problem on the most informal basis and with as little outside help as possible.

Jesus' comments in Matthew 18:15-17 sketch a process of dealing with those in need of correction that precisely agrees with the procedure recommended above. But the apostle Paul made the main point best, so far as the appropriate mood of administrative correction is involved, when he wrote not only to ministers but to all Christians: "Brethren, if a man is overtaken in any trespass, you who are spiritual should restore him in a spirit of gentleness" (Gal. 6:1).

So abide these three—goal setting, staffing, and administration. Upon them, so far as the parish church is concerned, largely depend the success or failure of all that will be covered in the following chapters. Yet goal setting, staffing, and administration are neglected subjects in most theological seminaries. Few ministers have experience or training in them before entering upon their first pastorates. Even fewer opportunities exist by which this lack can afterward be repaired. Nevertheless, every minister who accepts the full charge of a local congregation is thereby ordained the resident expert in all three. It is therefore hoped the foregoing, which has come to me out of the wisdom of more experienced ministers and the pain of my own errors, may assist other clergy in avoiding some of the parish minister's worst administrative mistakes! And, for what cannot be avoided, at least make most of the lumps little ones.

The Public Worship of God

Worship entered the English language by way of the Anglo-Saxon word "weorthscipe," which later was amended to "worthsip" or "worthship." As the latter spelling suggests, "worship" describes the action of attributing worth to something, and its original applications extended far beyond the religious sphere. But the religious connotation alone is of interest to us here; and within that discipline, we find the threefold implications of "bowing down before," "singing the praises of," and "bringing offerings or service" to God. The psalter, often referred to as the hymnbook of the apostolic church, is of great assistance at this point. Psalms 95, 96, and 100 present clear outlines of what worship meant to Jesus and to those who wrote the New Testament. Thus with reference to humankind's proper subservience, we read: "O come, let us worship and bow down, let us kneel before the Lord, our Maker! For he is our God, and we are the people of his pasture, and the sheep of his hand" (Ps. 95:6-7). Or again, speaking of the praise, offerings, and service that are God's due: "Ascribe to the Lord the glory due his name; bring an offering, and come into his courts!" (Ps. 96:8). "Make a joyful noise to the Lord, all the lands! Serve the Lord with gladness! Come into his presence with singing!" (Ps. 100:1).

But one day, outside the Samaritan city of Sychar, our Lord

delivered the final Christian word on the worship of God. His audience consisted of a single Samaritan woman of dubious reputation. This lady, being angered by Jesus' criticism of her moral conduct, sought to entangle him in that ageless debate as to which particular religious sect or communion actually worships God in the way he desires. The specific issue she raised was whether God wanted to be worshiped after the Samaritan fashion on Mount Gerizim, or according to the Judean ritual on Jerusalem's Mount Zion. Jesus' answer given in these familiar sentences, exposes the only devotion that ever pleases our Father in heaven, as well as the ultimate test as to whether any particular office belongs in the public worship of God or not:

> The hour is coming, and now is, when the true worshipers will worship the Father in spirit and truth, for such the Father seeks to worship him. God is spirit, and those who worship him must worship in spirit and truth. (John 4:23-24)

Lately, serious church watchers (and particularly parish-church watchers) have concluded that the coming hour at last now is. An end to two thousand years of Christian bickering over what properly constitutes the public worship of God just may be in sight. Christians everywhere seem on the verge of foregoing divisiveness in favor of worshiping the Father as one undivided Body of Christ, "in spirit and truth." That is the view held here. Therefore, in what follows, the central activity of any authentic Christian community—the public worship of God—will be discussed under three headings: the church's liturgy, planning the public worship of God, and the preparation of a sermon.

The Church's Liturgy

Liturgy, at least since the Apostolic Age, has designated "the act of taking part in the solemn corporate worship of God by the 'priestly' society of Christians, who are 'the Body of Christ,' the Church."[1] Or to say the same thing another way, the Greek word that translates into the English word "liturgy" actually means "work of the people" or "the people's work" (Acts 13:2).

Several terribly significant considerations derive from these circumstances. To begin with, the church's liturgy is to be thought of as work and not entertainment. All baptized Christians are expected to take part in its accomplishment. The church's liturgy cannot, without contradicting its central meaning, be left to a salaried professional minister, assisted by a salaried professional organist and a semiprofessional choir. Neither can the church's liturgy be confined to Sundays alone. It is a total seven days per week labor, required of the entire Christian comunity—to be conducted in the parish sanctuary but also in all the different places Christians live and work and play.

These preliminary considerations lead to what may be regarded as the only proper definition of the church's liturgy. Very early in the Christian era, "the first day of the week" (John 20:1, 19, 26), or Sunday, became the Lord's Day, the occasion on which the weekly celebration of Christ's Easter resurrection from the dead took place. Saturday, the Jewish Sabbath, had long been the seventh, or last, day of the week, on which both God and his entire creation rested (Gen. 2:2). The Jewish Sabbath and the Christian Lord's Day are frequently mentioned in the New Testament, and the earliest Jewish Christian communities customarily observed both (from which practice eventually derived our modern two-day weekend). But in time, especially after Gentile Christian congregations came to outnumber the original Jewish Christian communities, Christian religious observances on the Jewish Sabbath were dropped. So the church eventually came to its present two-part understanding of her liturgy; wherein, on the first day of the week, the people's work consists of celebrating the public worship of God in God's house with prayers, hymns, lessons, a sermon, an offering, and the Lord's Supper; while on each of the last six days of the week, the people's work consists of doing the church's mission out in God's world. So John Skoglund writes:

> Liturgy . . . basically means a "work of the people." This work is performed not only in terms of ritual acts but also in the

> world. . . . Worship cannot be identified solely with one Sunday hour of quiet meditation, separated from the world, but must instead be seen as the whole work of the people of God, both as they pray and as they engage themselves in the hard struggles of the world.[2]

Indeed what happens (or at least what ought to happen) at Lord's Day worship, on each Sunday morning in every parish church, assumes its proper meaning only when Lord's Day worship and six days of Christian mission following it are seen as inseparable parts of a single Christian liturgy!

Turning then to the narrow issue of what a Christian congregation ought to be about at public worship on the Lord's Day, we find in W. D. Maxwell's *Outline of Christian Worship* these introductory sentences on the two essential parts of that particular rite:

> Christian worship, as a distinctive, indigenous thing, arose from the fusion, in the crucible of Christian experience of the synagogue and the Upper Room. . . . The typical worship of the Church is to be found to this day in the union of the worship of the synagogue and the sacramental experience of the Upper Room; and that union dates from New Testament times.[3]

From the synagogue the church derived its service of the Word; from the Upper Room its service of the Sacrament. Both are rooted in Judaism, were celebrated by Jesus, and have been conveyed by our Lord as sacred obligations upon his followers. But over all the centuries since, powerful and conflicting forces reshaped this original inheritance, until by the middle of the twentieth century, a bewildering number of Lord's Day liturgies were in use, and the Christian church had splintered into dozens of warring sects over the question of what was authentic Christian worship—and what was not.

Then in the early 1960s, just as the American civil order began to come apart, the American church took a giant stride toward coming together. Riding a mood of ecumenism set in motion by Pope John XXIII, the Commission on Worship of the Consultation on Church Union (COCU), published a common Lord's Day liturgy, based upon exhaustive study of scripture and Christian tradition, which was subsequently adapted, approved, and placed in use by most of the major communions of the American church. It therefore is the conviction here that any parish church that does not shape its Sunday worship in accordance with this design inflicts upon both present and future Christians an unacceptable estrangement from their true Christian inheritance and the whole Body of Christ.

For that reason, this discussion of the church's Lord's Day worship, where components are examined, will focus on the forms and nomenclature appearing in the COCU common liturgy.

Our Christian Lord's Day liturgy has always moved on two levels—that of drama and that of words. So far as drama is concerned, congregations make their primary liturgical decision in the design of their sanctuary, because any sancturary is really a stage, especially designed and constructed for acting out, in a certain way, the public worship of God.

Given the many different shapes in which church sanctuaries have been laid out over the centuries, only the primary Western church architectural form can be discussed here. In the traditional split-chancel Christian sanctuary, a handful of design features are of principal importance. The narthex (sometimes called the vestibule) is the point of connection between God's world, where the Christian liturgy as God's Mission is carried on, and God's house, where the congregation gathers on the first day of each week to celebrate Christ's Easter resurrection from the dead. The chancel, standing at the opposite end of the sanctuary and connected to the narthex by an aisle, is the "holy of holies" or "the place where God is." The chancel is separated from the nave, which contains pews for the congregation, by three ascending steps, signifying the cardinal virtues of faith, hope, and love, and contains the lectern, pulpit, Bible, communion table or altar, candles, chancel cross, and choir stalls.

Mention needs to be made of vestments. Whatever costume the choir, clergy, and lay readers wear during the conduct of public worship, it ought to be consistent with the architecture of the sanctuary, the character of the service, and the particular ecclesiastical tradition in which both stand. No sensible person would attempt to put on *Hamlet* in a stage setting designed for *The Man Who Came to Dinner* with a cast costumed for *Oklahoma.* But this kind of mindless incongruity in the Sunday morning worship services of Protestant America is far more the rule than the exception.

So far as actors in the drama are concerned, the choir is of crucial importance. In the traditional Lord's Day service, it always represents the congregation. Thus, during the processional hymn, when the choir moves out of the narthex into the chancel, which is to say out of the world and into the holy of holies, it symbolically moves the congregation into the presence of God. And with the recessional hymn, when the choir leaves the chancel for the narthex, it returns the congregation to the world and the Christian mission again.

The minister as actor, in congregations affirming the priesthood of all believers, is considerably less important than the choir. In communions such as the Roman Catholic and the Anglican, which convey a unique priestly function on a separated clergy, just the reverse is the case. It therefore is ironic that those parts of the American church which argue most strongly against a special priesthood should have been and remain the communities of faith most prone to turn the public worship of God into a nonparticipatory "one-man show," conducted by a professional orator who gets the worship out of the way in twenty minutes or less so he or she can deliver a twenty-five to forty-minute sermon placed, solely for dramatic impact, just before the end of the service. Anglican and Roman Catholic services, despite the presence of a special priesthood, have always required much more participation by the congregation, have never permitted their clergy to conduct a one-man show, and thereby have maintained the Lord's Day liturgy as much more a work of the people.

The Lord's Day liturgy, as words, provides the script for the drama just rehearsed. In bare-bones outline, the salient features of the new common liturgy, as published in the Consultation on Church Union Proposal,[4] are: "The Greeting," in which the congregation is called out of the world to enter upon public worship and God's presence is invoked; "An Act of Praise," always corporate and involving a hymn of praise or psalm; "An Act of Penitence," consisting of a call to confession, a corporate prayer of confession, and words of absolution, uttered on God's behalf by the presiding cleric; "The Proclamation of the Word of God," consisting of the reading of scripture lessons and the preaching of a sermon based upon them (after the example of the Jewish synagogue); "The Prayers," offered by the minister but always in the name of the congregation, and chiefly consisting of petitions and intercessions; "The Offertory," being the supreme act of rededication by the congregation, in which the parish's "tithes and offerings" are presented, after which a hymn of thanksgiving is often sung and the Lord's Prayer is corporately offered; "The Lord's Supper," involving elements brought forward with the offering, a prayer of consecration, the scriptural words of institution, distribution to the congregation, and prayers of thanksgiving (after the example of the upper room); and "The Dismissal," consisting of the benediction and a charge to go out into the world and enter again upon the Christian mission. At services where the Lord's Supper is not celebrated, the order of worship moves directly from the Offertory to the Dismissal.

Several footnotes need to be appended to these all too brief observations on the church's liturgy.

Music—congregational, choral, and instrumental—is indispensable to effective public worship. As the Bible reveals, the Apostolic Church inherited a rich tradition of religious music from Judaism (Psalms 149 and 150), which she immediately began to elaborate and expand in ways of her own. The subject of church music is, however, far too vast to be treated here. But what can be noted is that good church music only ought to be used; individual selections and the times of their appearance should contribute to the particular part of the service they grace; and virtuoso performances, inserted for entertainment value only, should be scrupulously avoided.

As to flexibility and innovation—within the bare-bones

order of worship outline offered above, unlimited possibilities for variation and denominational uniqueness exist, without disturbing the progression of the principal units. Thus, to change the metaphor, like the mustard seed that "grows up and becomes greatest of all shrubs, and puts forth large branches" (Mark 4:32), the new common liturgy has proved roomy enough that all the various communions in the American church have so far been able to nest comfortably among its ample branches.

A word of caution needs to be directed to those congregations which only infrequently celebrate the Lord's Supper, as well as to those which, while celebrating the Lord's Supper constantly, give only indifferent attention to the proclamation of God's Word. Either distortion drastically diminishes the effectiveness of Christian public worship and should be avoided.

And finally a suggestion: any clergyman with the courage to undertake a three or four-month period of experimentation with his or her congregation and the new common liturgy will be presented with an unparalleled opportunity to instruct Christians in the meaning of the public worship of God, will thereby truly make liturgy the people's work, and—best of all—will end up with a style of public worship most agreeable to the tastes of his or her particular congregation, that nevertheless represents a bonafide extension of a tradition that began in the first-century synagogues of Palestine and in Maundy Thursday's Upper Room.

Planning the Public Worship of God

Here is a much neglected labor whose proper accomplishment will immediately improve the quality of parish public worship, permit infinitely more preciseness and variety in the materials employed, and contribute immensely to both the preacher's and music director's peace of mind.

The problems attendant upon planning the public worship of God are not new. The original Christian communities faced three major deficiencies in their efforts to accomplish this task—an uneducated clergy, an illiterate laity, and an extreme shortage of Bibles. But in a marvelous way, necessity proved the mother of invention. Each of these deficiencies was triumphantly overcome. And the church emerged from her tribulations not only alive and well but also with the finest instrument of Christian education ever produced. That is the tale that now needs to be told.

Full texts of the Bible being unavailable, since Gutenberg did not introduce movable type to Western Europe until the fifteenth century, the early Christian communities customarily sent off some local scholar to the nearest Christian center where a full or partial text of Holy Writ was located. Certain specific passages, known as pericopes, or "portions cut around," were copied out and brought home. Neighboring parishes then exchanged secondary copies of their gleanings. And through this process of copying and swapping, local parish churches soon gathered comprehensive collections of pericopes that, in some sort of regular order, then became the appointed lessons to be read on each particular Sunday. Not the least of the contributions made by these pericopes was the influence they had on the final form of the New Testament. For pericopes were in general circulation several centuries before the canon was closed. What was found to be most helpful, inspiring, and doctrinally correct, in the experience of countless parish churches, therefore had a way of escaping the Apocrypha and ending up, together with the document from which it was drawn, in the church's New Testament.

But pericopes led immediately to another development. An uneducated clergy, serving widely scattered parish churches, could not be expected to know which parts of the bewildering and still growing body of Christian writings were important and which were not. So very early, major Christian centers and leading bishops began to circulate lists of scriptures appointed to be read on each Sunday of the year. These lists, which were also the product of extensive Christian parish experience, marked the beginning of formal lectionaries. Now a parish could know for certain what specific pericopes its scholars ought to copy, and its clergy would be equally clear as to what lessons should be read and expounded each Sunday and any other holy day of the year.

The final flowering of pericopes and lectionaries was the church year. Advent, Christmas, Epiphany, Lent, Easter, Ascension Day, Pentecost, Trinity, and all the lesser Christian holy days in between, now moved into permanent places on a twelve-month calendar. Each Lord's Day and every other holy occasion had Old and New Testament lessons appointed to be used as the basis for public worship. The homegrown clergyman who never attended a theological school was thereby afforded a sophisticated understanding of what he should be about at any given service. In the annually repeated passage of the Christian seasons, most of which were soon tied to secular events such as planting, harvesting, school openings, et cetera, the illiterate laity began to grasp a rudimentary outline of the Christian gospel. (To the same purpose, liturgical colors for each Christian season were developed. An unlettered Christian, merely by understanding a simple color code, could ascertain what his parish church was, on this or that occasion, celebrating.) The church year also quickly proved one of the major fountainheads of systematic theology. Indeed, its general impact on the development of Christian doctrine and Christian education was ever so much more powerful than anything else, because by the beginning of the fourth Christian century the church year was not simply thought about or discussed by a few learned persons but was actually acted out daily by Christians everywhere.

The Christian church year still consists, as it has from the beginning, of two semesters—"the Lord's half year" and "the church's half year." The former begins with the first Sunday in Advent and ends with the last day of Pentecost season. Over its course, God's mighty work of salvation in Jesus Christ—starting with the Annunciation and ending with the resurrected Christ commissioning his church—is completely elaborated, lived through, and acted out. Actually, every major Christian holiday appears somewhere in the Lord's half year. The church's half year begins with Trinity Sunday and ends on the Saturday immediately preceding the first Sunday in Advent. Often called Trinity Season, the church's half year is devoted entirely to Christian growth and churchmanship.

Not a single major Christian holiday distrubs its flow. But in the American church, its span includes school summer vacation, harvest season, and those beautiful autumn weekends before those urban and suburban Christians who can enjoy such pleasures put up their boats, abandon the beaches, and close their summer cottages. All of which leads to a very practical consideration that is fundamental to the proper planning of public worship.

The majority of American parish churches, so far as attendance at public worship is concerned, enjoy a one-semester year. Not too long ago, this condition led many Protestant parishes to close down entirely over the summer months. Happily that solution has since been generally rejected. But what is demanded of the parish minister by Christian Americans' summer life-style is some sort of an adjustment involving the parts of the Christian curriculum that are supposed to be covered during the church's half year, when only a fraction of one's parish will be attending Lord's Day worship, and the meticulous observation and celebration of all major events in the Lord's half year. This task is further complicated by the fact that certain dates from the civil or secular calendar—such as Thanksgiving Sunday, Brotherhood Sunday, Race Relations Sunday, et cetera—need to be worked into the Lord's half year as well.

But none of these problems is insurmountable. The parish minister can effect an excellent result if he or she will do two things: avoid being slavishly bound to any lectionary, and plan the parish's services of public worship well in advance.

Concerning lectionaries, seminary professors have long advised their students to preach the church year, strictly following a lectionary, for the first three to five years of ministry. That remains excellent advice. Given the church year's educative capabilities, there are few better ways for a young minister to familiarize himself or herself with the whole round of the gospel, to expand his or her knowledge of the great events in the history of the people of God, or to firm up a proper understanding of biblical theology.

But lectionaries are limiting. None covers the whole Bible

or even all that is important. Each has a theological bias that in no way embraces the total substance of Holy Writ. Therefore any minister who attempts to be an expository preacher while strictly adhering to a lectionary will soon find himself or herself preaching on the same selections of scripture again and again, at the expense of other parts of God's Word, which are never touched. After the minister's homiletical apprenticeship is over, he is therefore urged to exercise considerable but judicious freedom in selecting the lessons to be read and expounded at Lord's Day worship. The proper themes of the Christian seasons and holy days must never be ignored. However, as the minister becomes more experienced, he or she should be able, in the spirit of the Pilgrim pastor John Robinson, who had confidence that "God has more light and truth to break forth from His holy Word," to draw treasures both old and new out of the Bible that will enrich rather than diminish the educative influence of the Christian church year.

As to the practicalities of planning public worship, the parish minister ought to develop the schedule of services with the responsible lay leadership (probably the deacons and deaconesses) and involved staff members, a semester at a time and well in advance of the first celebration. This will be most expeditiously accomplished if the parish minister creates the full proposal for later discussion and confirmation. And the best way of going about that is as follows: (1) prepare a dummy calendar, showing each Sunday and other holy day; (2) designate all special Sundays and holy days, such as First in Advent, Race Relations Sunday, Church School Day; (3) note on the dummy calendar the dates on which baptisms, confirmations, the Lord's supper, family Sundays, and musical services will be offered; and (4) proceed with the actual planning of individual services. Respecting the final step, lessons are selected, the sermon text chosen, the sermon title devised, and—if more than one minister handles the preaching—the name of the one responsible is placed against each indicated service date. (Obviously, the designated preacher for a given Sunday's sermon will select the lessons, text, and title.)

This semester-long schedule should then be discussed with

and published to the board of deacons and deaconesses, the staff, and the congregation. It thereafter will be adhered to, except as collectively adjusted to meet unforeseen eventualities. My experience, over two decades of following this practice, has been that changes other than minor ones are almost never required. I recall only four events—the assassinations of Martin Luther King, John F. Kennedy, and Robert Kennedy; and the Cuban missile crisis—that necessitated the complete scrapping of a planned service. In each instance, an emergency staff meeting was called. A new order of worship was designed and published, different lessons were chosen, and a new sermon was written. In the case of Dr. King's assassination, which occurred on the Thursday before Palm Sunday of 1968, the last touch was applied to the sermon just as dawn was breaking and the choir arrived at the church to begin rehearsing the as yet unfamiliar anthems they would present to an overflow Palm Sunday congregation a few hours later.

Before leaving this subject, because of its overriding importance to the quality of any parish's public worship, I offer these five observations on the virtues of such planning:

1. Advance planning of an entire semester's services of public worship enables the minister to take an overview of what he is about, permits the devising of sermon series, prevents homiletical redundancy, and allows for a balanced offering of both public and personal religion.

2. Sharing such a schedule with other professional staff members, particularly with the director of music, permits a far better quality of church music to be used; the musical offerings can be much more thoroughly rehearsed; hymns truly appropriate to a particular service may be selected; and a collective and far more consistent supporting liturgy can be developed (particularly if more than one minister participates in the service).

3. Publishing a semester-long schedule of services in advance allows other parish program organizations, such as the Christian education and the mission committees, to relate their efforts directly to what is going on at this particular moment or that in public worship.

4. Publishing a semester-long schdule of services in advance allows the laity, particularly the board of deacons and

deaconesses, to become personally involved in the production of public worship, thereby enabling them to appreciate in a far more serious way that doing the church's liturgy really is the people's work.

5. The parish minister who has done this kind of planning, and hence possesses lessons, texts, and sermon titles for each Sunday of the entire semester, is thereby forever relieved of the Tuesday-morning jitters about "what shall I preach next Sunday?" and usually the Saturday-night struggle to get the sermon done.

The Preparation of a Sermon

After 1919 and the publication of Martin Dibelius' *From Tradition to Gospel,* a great truth about preaching dawned upon Christendom. Dibelius' study proved that, to a very considerable extent, the New Testament and particularly the Gospels were written out of the sermon manuscripts of the Apostolic Church.[5] An oral tradition preceded all else. In the guise of cult stories, sermons, legends, and exhortations, these verbalizations of earliest Christian faith and life soon assumed set forms. Preacher passed them to preacher. They were polished and refined, so as to deal with the full range of a Christian's personal religious needs and those of the church's mission. Then came personal notes and circular letters to the churches which were similarly shaped and improved. Eventually, but not before many of these units of tradition had been in Christian service for at least a quarter century, they found their way into the Gospels and Epistles of the New Testament.

The point of recalling these developments here is to lay a foundation for understanding the source and substance of authentic Christian preaching. The Bible is always its only proper source. Any proper Christian sermon, despite its internal design and purpose, will be expository. Indeed, in the light of what has just been rehearsed, it is not too much to suggest that the primary task of a modern Christian preacher is to take some part of the apostolic proclamation, spread on the pages of the Bible, and offer its substance in application to the needs of Christians and the world today.

Nothing in the foregoing, however, is intended to suggest

that the preacher ought to ignore the Old Testament, which is also the Word of God, was Jesus' Bible, and actually went through the same process of formulation as the Gospels and Epistles. The central point to be grasped is that, in all of Christian preaching, the minister is expected to take some portion of the biblical Word of God and apply it as a "living and active . . . two-edged sword, piercing to the division of soul and spirit, of joints and marrow" (Heb. 4:12) to God's work in the world today.

The other principal argument for expository preaching resides in the fact that Christianity's "service of the Word" comes directly from the practice of the first-century Jewish synagogue, of which the central feature was a public reading or readings from the Old Testament, followed by a homily based upon these lessons, delivered by a qualified rabbi or teacher. These verses from the Third Gospel perfectly describe the Jewish rite, as it was observed by Jesus and continued in the Apostolic Church:

> and [Jesus] went to the synagogue, as his custom was, on the sabbath day. And he stood up to read; and there was given to him the book of the prophet Isaiah. He opened the book and found the place where it was written,
> "The Spirit of the Lord is upon me,
> because he has anointed me to preach good news to the poor.
> He has sent me to proclaim release to the captives
> and recovering of sight to the blind,
> to set at liberty those who are oppressed,
> to proclaim the acceptable year of the Lord."
> And he closed the book, and gave it back to the attendant, and sat down; and the eyes of all in the synagogue were fixed on him. And he began to say to them, "Today this scripture has been fulfilled in your hearing." (Luke 4:16-21)

John Calvin, purely on the basis of Jesus' example, returned a wandering church to her still current definition of the sermon as "a passage of scripture and a homily expounding it." In fact, the great reformer took the importance of unadulterated expository preaching so seriously that he would have no lectionaries, condemned the church year as a man-made distortion of God's Word, and habitually preached through the books of the Old and New Testaments in course.

So much by way of establishing the Christian sermon's standpoint and purpose. Now to the practicalities of producing one. Any clergyman who would fulfill his or her preaching responsibilities properly needs to be prepared to expend ten to fifteen hours of hard work each week on sermon preparation. Harry Emerson Fosdick's standard of one hour in preparation for each minute in the pulpit remains a fair measure of the time a serious preacher needs to invest in preparing his or her weekly sermons. And there are no shortcuts. As Fosdick's great contemporary, Paul Scherer, used to tell his homiletic classes, "Good preaching is 5 percent genius, 10 percent inspiration, and 85 percent hard work."

But time and commitment alone are never enough. Five basic tools or resources are essential to the production of consistently superior sermons. These are (1) an adequate professional library, which needs to be constantly augmented, ideally with the help of a church-supplied book allowance; (2) a regular study program, made posible by a proper weekly schedule, the understanding of one's parish, and occasional sabbaticals or extended study periods for concentrated application; (3) a comprehensive yet efficient filing system, wherein the fruits of one's scholarly labors may be easily stored and readily recovered; (4) an active pastoral ministry, which alone can focus God's Word upon those situations and sorrows which, on this particular Sunday or that, need his grace most; and (5) a serious professional devotional life, sufficient to make each sermon not an essay in oratory but rather an exercise of prayer.

We now consider the individual steps involved in preparation of an actual sermon. What follows is by no means my own creation. Rather, it represents techniques presented to various homiletical classes and seminars, in three different seminaries, by four of the greatest expository preachers of the twentieth century. Of these, the major influence upon the discussion is that of Paul Scherer, late Brown Professor of Homiletics at the Union Theological Seminary in New York City:

(1) The Exegesis. An exhaustive study of the scripture lessons that are to undergird the sermon is the essential first step in sermon preparation. The preacher should begin by making a verse-by-verse, if not word-by-word, examination of each lesson, without reference to commentaries or any other secondary sources. He or she should constantly seek insights as to what particular words, phrases, or themes suggest in both their original and present historical context. These revelations will be carefully recorded on a work sheet devised for that purpose. Next, commentaries and other technical tools are consulted for additional information and insights, which will likewise be set down on the work sheet. Only after an adequate understanding of what the lessons mean in terms of themselves and sufficient insight into their present application have been gained will the exegetical effort be concluded.

(2) The Outline. A limited selection of ideas from the diverse and unconnected insights surfaced by the exegesis now need to be reduced to an orderly outline. If a sermon title and text have previously been chosen, they will shape the eventual result. The outline will consist of an introduction and either two or three points, more than that number being extremely difficult for the congregation to keep in mind or recall. These points, or "heads" as they used to be termed, need to be exclusive, and each should move the central sermon theme forward toward its final resolution. Selecting and shaping the sermon points or heads out of the welter of ideas produced by the exegesis is usually the most difficult yet crucial step in the production of a good expository sermon. Before undertaking this task, the sermon title is written down at the top of a clean page of legal-sized paper, and the sermon text inscribed beneath it. Along the left-hand border, below the sermon text, the word "Introduction" should be placed and, at descending one-third page intervals, the sermon points should be fully written out. Next, three subheadings at equal intervals in the space available below each sermon point will be noted—"Expansion," "Application," "Illustration." (If, as is sometimes the case, only a single sermon illustration is to be employed, "Illustration" will be inserted only as a sub-

heading below the last point). Filling in the space titled "Introduction" should always be left until last, since only after one has a sermon completely outlined is it clear what needs to be introduced. Now the subheadings under each of the sermon points are elaborated. Under "Expansion," the point will be developed in terms of its biblical background and fundamental meaning. Under "Application," the point will be related to a particular circumstance in the world or in the lives of those addressed. Under "Illustration," some anecdote or narrative that illuminates the central meaning and application of the point, will be transferred from the file or the preacher's experience to the sermon outine. But in all this developing of subheadings, the principle of parallelism will be kept in mind. This is to say, if the preacher elaborates each point in the same way, in approximately the same amount, and out of similar types of material, he or she thereby conveys an order upon the final result that will make the sermon infinitely easier for those in the pew to follow.

(3) The Manuscript. If the sermon outline has been adequately worked up, writing the sermon is relatively easy. George Buttrick used to sweat all week over a meticulous sermon outline, worked out on an intricate and detailed work sheet of his own devising. Then on Saturday night, after supper, he put his typewriter on the kitchen table and polished off the finished manuscript in a few hours. Although few of us can muster such superior organizational talents, the value of a solid sermon outline is clearly demonstrated in this great Presbyterian preacher's practice. In point of fact, when a minister has trouble pulling a sermon together, the most common cause of his or her difficulty is that the sermon outline was either incompletely or badly executed. Be this as it may, the sermon manuscript should be little more than a fleshing out of the sermon outline. It ought to be produced by the means with which its author feels most creatively comfortable—pencil, typewriter, or dictaphone. And it ought to be triple-spaced. The reason for the last injunction is two-fold. In the first draft, triple-spacing provides ample space for corrections, additions, deletions, and editing; without such alterations a polished final product cannot be produced. In

the final draft, triple-spacing produces a manuscript that will allow the preacher's eyes to function far more efficiently when visual prompting during the delivery of the sermon is required.

The preacher needs also to remember that the sermon is but a single part of the service, and the congregation's interest span has limits. Fifteen to twenty-five minutes, or six to eight triple-spaced typewritten pages, are enough.

(4) The Presentation. It is the opinion here that every preacher ought to take his or her full sermon manuscript into the pulpit. Some day, having it in the pulpit will prevent an embarrassing "blank." Yet of far more importance, working from a full manuscript permits the preacher to deliver the felicitous phrase or the sparkling quotation exactly as it stands in the final draft of the sermon.

But sermons are meant to be preached, not read. All of which requires the full-manuscript preacher to spend considerable time—possibly even extra time—in preparing a sermon for delivery. Beginners do well to rehearse their homily while standing in front of a bathroom or bedroom mirror, with their sermon manuscript resting on a makeshift platform, raised to the height of the sanctuary pulpit by dictionaries, encyclopedias, or telephone books. The mirror greatly assists one in learning to establish and maintain eye contact with the congregation, without losing sight of one's manuscript. More experienced preachers commonly accomplish the same thing by getting off by themselves an hour or so before the service, and carefully reading through the sermon mauscript three or four times.

If a preacher conscientiously follows the whole process outlined above, from the initial exegesis to preparation for delivery, he or she will soon be able to preach—not read—the sermon, and all of its best lines, just when needed, will be right there on the end of the tongue.

I conclude this chapter with a judgment out of the writings of Paul Scherer, whose understanding not only of preaching but also of Christian worship has been an ever-increasing support to my professional ministry, since I first sat in his homiletic classes a quarter century ago. Speaking of what he calls his two overriding "convictions" about the public worship of God, Scherer writes:

> One of them is that to the ever-changing panorama of the years the Word of God, properly understood, never has to be made relevant. Too much honest, misguided toil has been devoted to that. The Word of God is already relevant. It was relevant before we arrived on the scene. The honest toil is called for as one seeks to understand it, and by understanding to apprehend its relevance. All it asks is that instead of being adjusted to the modern situation, or exploited to ends it never had in mind, it be allowed to address, at this time and in this place, what is most deeply characteristic of human existence.
>
> The other unshaken conviction is that there is not today, there never has been, and there never will be any adequate substitute for preaching. The correspondence between the greatness or the wretchedness of the whole Christian enterprise, when one rightly conceives of them, and the fidelity or faithlessness of the Christian pulpit is, from age to age, altogether too obvious for anybody to miss it."[6]

The Teaching Ministry of the Parish Church

Christian education has always been a full-time occupation of every parish church. It goes on, for better or worse, whether clergy and laity are aware of that fact or not. Indeed, everything a parish church does—public worship, Christian mission, church school, music program, every-member canvass, social activities, et cetera—involves a teaching ministry and/or an exercise in Christian education. The purpose of this chapter is therefore to raise this essential office to a suitable level of consciousness by setting forth a modern, comprehensive program of Christian education capable of fulfilling the responsibilities of an authentic parish-church teaching ministry.

As has been the case since the Apostolic Age, the Christian teaching ministry begins with preparation for Christian baptism. Originally only adults were involved, an extensive period of preparation preceded the sacrament, and what the church now accomplishes in the sacrament or office of confirmation was included within it. The would-be Christian was commonly known as a catechumen. Until baptism, which was by immersion, he or she was not allowed to participate in the entire Lord's Day liturgy, the Lord's Supper being denied catechumens. Baptism was uniformly believer's baptism. The catechumen confessed his or her faith before the congregation by reciting a baptismal credo (these credos were the earliest confessions of faith owned by the church) and then was immersed in running water, signifying the dying of the old person and the birth of the new. So the apostle records the original practice: "We were buried therefore with him by baptism into death, so that as Christ was raised from the dead, by the glory of the Father, we too might walk in newness of life" (Rom. 6:4).

Among major American communions, the original practice is most faithfully preserved by the Baptists. Following the personal example of Jesus, as well as that of the earliest Jewish Christian communities, that communion celebrates a service of infant dedication, patterned on the experience of Jesus in the Temple during the first days of his life (Luke 2:22-40), followed by the ordinance of baptism, always administered after a period of instruction, the child having attained the age of discretion. The precedent for this office is the baptism of Jesus in the Jordan River by John the Baptist (Mark 1:9-11).

However, the largest part of the Christian church performs the sacrament of baptism as soon after birth as possible, substituting the faith of the parents and/or godparents for the faith of the infant. Then the office or sacrament of confirmation is offered after a course of instruction when the child is old enough to make an intelligent decision for Christ. When babies are baptized, the rite almost always is by sprinkling. The original rite's use of running water, implied now in sprinkling, symbolized the washing clean of sin, rather than the death and rebirth symbolized by going under and emerging from the water.

This later form—baptism followed by confirmation—also has ancient and biblical precedents. Those communions arguing for the origins of their practice in the Apostolic Age cite the procedures followed after "Samaria had received the Word of God" (Acts 8:14-17) and what many New Testament scholars believe to have been Jesus' Bar Mitzvah, which Jews also speak of as "confirmation" (Luke 2:41-52), as equally solid grounds for their sacraments and ordinances.

But the common factor underlying these tedious arguments respecting the proper forms of baptism and/or confirmation is that all communions of the American church observe two rites between birth and the assumption of full adult membership in a parish church. The first contains solemn pledges by the congregation, the parents, sponsors, and godparents that they will do all in their power to supply the physical and personal needs of the infant, that they will so love the child as to convey assurance that a loving heavenly Father watches over all his or her earthly ways, that they will pray with and for the child, and that they will provide the child with an adequate Christian education.

The second rite, always taking place after the child's attainment of the age of discretion and usually somewhere between his or her twelfth and fourteenth year, is preceded by a period of special education and preparation for full church membership. At the end of the educative process and prior to performance of this second ritual, the requirement is that the child willingly, knowledgeably, and apart from any outside coercion elects to become a disciple of Jesus and member of the Body of Christ.

With the celebration of the second rite, be it believer's baptism or confirmation, the special responsibility of parents, godparents, and sponsors for their particular children is discharged. But the responsibility of the congregation, represented by the presence of deacons and deaconesses at private baptisms and by the pledge of all present church members at public baptisms, continues in force. This latter pledge is the foundation of the teaching ministry of the parish church. For every time a child is baptized in a particular congregation, that community's members, in the pledges they affirm, thereby recommit themselves to the Christian education enterprise on behalf of all the parish's children. In practical terms, the modern American congregation's obligations include every adult church member's promise to assist perpetually in the Christian education of all the parish's children, whether by accepting volunteer positions as church-school teachers and youth advisers or simply by supporting with their gifts the parish budget.

These circumstances lead directly to the duty of each parish church to publish and maintain an up-to-date church-school responsibility list. The children of every parish family, whether or not they ever come near the church, belong on that list. For in total, the young people named on the parish's church-school responsibility list constitute that religious community's minimal obligation, before God and his Christ, for the Christian education of children. Concerning this roster, the church school's responsibility list ought at least to cover all parish children from the time of birth through the age of confirmation. Beyond this, it is an excellent idea to maintain lists of post-confirmation high-school and college-age young people. The names on the church-school responsibility list should be broken down into groupings that coincide with the young people's grade in public school. Children who have been left back or prematurely advanced need to be assigned on the basis of their best interests. After the child is confirmed, it is a wise idea, from a Christian education standpoint, to treat him or her as an adult. Some accommodation to adolescence, especially a high quality senior high youth fellowship, ought to be implemented. But it is an excellent idea to let confirmed young people participate as fully as possible in the adult activities of the parish—particularly in adult education opportunities, parish committee and board responsibilities, and stewardship.

On this latter head, there has long been an unnecessary inconsistency involved in granting full church membership to thirteen- or fourteen-year-olds that ought to be erased. For while confirmed young people are usually granted access to the communion table and certain minimal membership privileges, the corporation laws of most states forbid their voting on budgets, property transfers, the election or dismissal of ministers, and changes in the parish by-laws until they reach the legal age of maturity, which is eighteen. Not only does much unhappiness result from this restriction, but also a great Christian education opportunity is missed.

Some years back, in a precedent-setting move, the Protestant churches of Massachusetts successfully petitioned the legislature to amend that state's corporation laws to exempt parish churches from maturity requirements. Each parish was given the right to establish, in its own parish by-laws, the age at which confirmed young people would receive full legal rights respecting the business affairs of the congregation. At once, most of that state's Protestant parishes amended their parish by-laws to allow full privileges in all business affairs, regardless of age, to any confirmed member of the church. Despite a spate of dire predictions, the practice has worked to perfection. No participating church has suffered harm, and many more young people have become fully involved, in at least one part of the adult world, years before they can enter any other. The Massachusetts precedent should be followed by all other states in the Union. Its adoption would immediately produce a marvelous advancement of the church's teaching ministry and a great step foward in Christian education.

We now turn directly to what constitutes the basic teaching ministry of a parish church in its effort to fulfill the congregation's baptismal promises to its children. The major activities are three—the church school, a family life or Christian life emphasis program, and a junior youth fellowship. Some discussion of the purpose, structure, and program of each will be offered.

A modern American parish church school, designed to serve children, will have a clearly defined and limited purpose. To begin with, it should look like, act like, and function as a school. Its youngest constituents will be preschool nursery youngsters. Its graduating seniors are those who, at age thirteen or fourteen, have completed the curriculum of the confirmation department; for it is the opinion here that confirmation study, of at least two years duration, should be an integral part and the capstone of the parish church school.

The aim of this Christian educational process, which begins in the nursery department and ends with the ninth grade (assuming this is the age at which young people either are confirmed or undergo believers' baptism), is to provide each child in the parish with a thorough grounding in Christian faith and life, particularly as it is revealed in the Bible and in church tradition. To this end, curriculum materials ought to be carefully selected on the basis of their substantive contribution to these purposes. A personal Bible, employing the text used by the parish church, ought to be presented to each child in a special service conducted as part of Sunday worship, on one of the first fall Sundays of his or her fourth-grade church-school year. This Bible must be viewed not as an attendance prize but rather as the principal textbook of the entire Christian education program. It should be presented to fourth graders, for they are the youngest students who can be expected to read from it themselves. It is good to present the Bibles on a fall Sunday morning instead of at Church-School Day in the spring, so that they may immediately be put to use, rather than gather dust over the summer. The child's Bible ought to be brought to church school and used in some sort of classroom experience on each and every Sunday. Failure to do this suggests to the child that the Bible is not important to one's Christian education.

In the preschool and early grades, larger classrooms, including a variety of learning centers, are desirable. Construction projects may be located in one corner, a storytelling center in another, games or a sandbox in another, and a piano or worship center in still another. Thus during the classroom session, the children may move, for different activities, to different program sites about the room. Multiple staff greatly facilitates this process. One teacher can be preparing the next event while another conducts the present one. In this fashion, the relatively short interest span of small children will not be overextended, and the learning experience will be infinitely more interesting and valuable for all concerned.

Older classes may be effectively located in somewhat smaller classrooms, set up about tables in seminar fashion. Row seating, with the teacher up front, does not encourage student participation, dialogue, or—in the long run—even attendance.

As to church school faculty, a modern team-teaching approach is, by any standard, the best. The ancient idea of each class having its teacher, with a pool of unprepared, usually reluctant, substitutes in the background, is a prescription for disaster. Teachers get worn out. Every

Sunday morning involves a last-minute frantic search for substitutes. And the overall effect on the students is deadly. A modern church-school teaching team consists of a lead teacher and four or five associate teachers. The lead teacher is in charge, under direction of the minister or the Christian educator, for implementing the board of Christian education's policy directives and for all class activities. The teaching team is responsible for the participation of each child on the Christian education responsibility list. The lead teacher arranges teacher-training sessions for the entire team, soliciting professional staff as resources or educational help are required; and the lead teacher also arranges curriculum and teacher schedules (i.e., what will be taught on which Sunday and which members of the teaching team will be responsible for leading a particular classroom session). The advantages of such a modern team-teaching approach to the overall performance of a parish church school are so compelling that a number of its more conspicuous virtues are listed here:

1. Recruiting is infinitely easier, because any particular teacher knows he or she will not have to work every Sunday and can get off whenever necessary. This flexibility also enables the recruitment of many more men, as well as busy people of superior skills, who under the older one-teacher–one-class system could not consider a year-long obligation.

2. Teacher training takes place naturally and in the process. More experienced teachers give on-the-job training to newer ones, and professional staff are provided with an unparalleled opportunity, without the need for arranging special teacher-training courses, to deal directly with front-line teachers at the point of their need.

3. Substitute pools or lists are unnecessary. If one teacher cannot meet a class, another teacher from the same team, already prepared and trained to do so, takes over.

4. If the church school is in session at the same time as morning worship, a practice followed by a steadily increasing number of American churches, no teacher is denied the chance to attend services regularly. Under the older system involving single teachers for each class, church-school

teachers often had no opportunity to attend their parish's public worship at all.

5. Teaching teams can be put together so as to include varieties of gifts. A storyteller, a piano player, a handicraft expert, a Bible scholar, and a song leader are not usually all found in the same church-school teacher. They can, however, be brought together in the same church-school teaching team.

6. Both the church-school teachers and students find team teaching considerably more enjoyable. The teachers do not get worn out. They find cooperation in common aims with other adults stimulating, and enjoy a positive experience in Christian service. The children find the resulting program to be much more interesting, are intrigued by the differing approaches of the adults making up the teaching team, and have the opportunity to become acquainted with a much larger group of the most dedicated adults in the church.

7. Student absenteeism and church-school dropouts can be much more effectively handled by a teaching team than by a single teacher. In the latter case, one overworked individual must do all the follow-up and, even when faithful in this formidable labor, often gets the reputation of being a nag. The teaching team divides the responsibility, assigns absentees to the team member whose concern may be the most effective, overloads no one, and conveys to the absentee and his or her parents a sense that not just one teacher but a whole group of parish adults are concerned about the student's Christian welfare.

Team teaching by lay persons ought to be carried through the seventh grade. When the student enters the confirmation department (which we would urge be of two years duration, followed by confirmation at the end of the ninth-grade year), a minister or other professional teacher is desirable. In multiple-staff churches, the associate minister often conducts this class over its entire two-year span. Where only a single cleric is available, a special professional teacher can be retained. Our confirmation department, taught by the associate minister, offers a revolving two-year program, one year being devoted to the Old Testament and the next to the New. Eighth and ninth graders take the same class together.

Seventy-five percent attendance, with make-up assignments for missed sessions, is required for confirmation. At present, we celebrate confirmation on Pentecost Sunday (which normally falls at the end of our parish church-school year) as part of regular morning worship. The church service is followed by a formal reception of the confirmands by the entire parish.

The family life or Christian life emphasis program is designed to provide young children in family groups valid experiences of Christian fellowship and growth within the parish community. Nine or ten different programs are offered each year. In our parish these have included all church picnics, an annual family weekend retreat, the hanging of the greens (a program in which our families decorate the interior of the church and parish house early each Advent), family-night suppers, all church Sunday luncheons, family bus trips to points of cultural and religious interest, and entertaining Christian drama and singing groups. A short while ago, we became aware that labeling these "family life" programs conveyed a connotation to older church members, widows, widowers, and unmarried Christians of all ages that they were not wanted. Upon correcting this misunderstanding, we discovered that young unmarried adults and senior citizens of all varieties are some of the most enthusiastic participants in these opportunities; and further that, without diminishing their value to small children—in fact increasing it—we could rename them "Christian life emphasis" programs and consciously make their thrust intergenerational. At the moment, that is what is being done.

Junior youth fellowships differ from senior youth fellowships in most churches principally in that the former involve young people who are not yet full adult church members, while the latter involve those who are.[1] Essentially the same concerns, staffing, and program—though adjusted to meet the needs respectively of early and late adolescence—are involved in each. Therefore, in the interest of saving space, this discussion will deal with the subject of parish youth fellowships in general.

As growing up in America has become more complicated,

the parish-church youth-fellowship program has been presented with new opportunities and new difficulties. The opportunities arise principally because, with the breaking down of neighborhood and community support systems and the diminished capability of families to guide, protect, and discipline adolescents, most Christian adults are today extremely interested in having their children involved in a serious Christian youth program. The difficulties, beyond the earlier loss of adult control over American young people, chiefly stem from the infinite number of alternative secular activities available to all but the very poor, between the ages of twelve and eighteen. Little league baseball, rocket football, competitive swimming, youth soccer leagues, hockey programs, the movies, television, and dating consume most of the average middle-class adolescent American's waking hours. Nationwide, schoolwork, as measured against such standards as the Scholastic Aptitude Tests, has suffered from this youth-oriented recreational onslaught as well. That means, if the parish youth program is to survive and flourish, it must appeal to both parents and young people on its merits alone as something which must be fitted into the young persons' and family's already overcrowded schedule. Our emphatic contention is that a properly conceived youth fellowship program can appeal and will be fitted into the schedules of most active parish families. The following discussion endeavors to demonstrate why.

First and foremost, the youth-fellowship program needs to be based on a clear conception of what it is in business to accomplish. If the church school's task is to teach the content of the biblical faith and Christian tradition to the parish young people, the youth fellowship's business is to assist in developing those social skills, qualities of character, life goals, and self-confidence which are essential to successful Christian living. To accomplish this formidable task, adequate staff, an effective process of program development and implementation, sufficient adult assistance, and a reasonable budget must be provided. Each of these will now be discussed in turn.

We argued earlier that either a minister or a specially trained and probably salaried professional teacher ought to conduct the parish's two-year confirmation program. The same high priority ought be given to staffing the youth-fellowship program. If at all possible, the person in charge should be a young minister whom the parish youth will regard as a friend, as a big brother or sister, and yet also as an authentic Christian minister. Parish churches fortunate enough to have an apprentice associate minister—assuming they have chosen one interested in and attractive to young people—are in the best position. The parish church with a single minister, and possibly an older one at that, ought to think about employing a theological student from a local seminary on a part-time basis. Excellent leadership is often supplied by a young, enthusiastic seminarian willing to give two to three days a week to the youth-fellowship program of a nearby church. Such arrangements are mutually beneficial, contributing both to the theological student's education and to the church's youth ministry. Indeed, such field-work experience is often required for graduation from divinity school. Should a seminarian not be available, the next best place to turn for part-time staff is to the teaching faculty of local junior high schools, senior high schools, or colleges. Often a young man or woman, and sometimes a young couple, can be secured who will supply inspired leadership. Such currently booming youth-fellowship programs as Young Life, Campus Crusade, Youth for Christ, and the Navigators are almost entirely staffed by young Christian lay people. The enthusiasm and organizational success they have recently generated testifies eloquently to the impressive achievements nonprofessional staff leadership can accomplish in the management of a Christian youth ministry.

However, these cautionary criteria need to be kept in mind if lay persons are employed to staff the youth program: (1) They need to be enthusiastic Christians; (2) they need to enjoy and be gifted in working with young people; (3) they must be emotionally stable, mature adults; (4) they should possess formal teaching, group-process, and recreational skills; and (5) they should be salaried.

On the latter head, the parish minister whose lay youth worker is salaried will save himself or herself a great deal of grief. A formal reporting arrangement and the parish minister's ultimate authority over the youth program will then be established. Far better performance can be expected. Staff leadership absenteeism will be greatly diminished. And finally, the youth participants, the congregation, and the staff member involved will recognize, because it is salaried, that the position of parish youth director is one of status and importance.

Program development and implementation are where most youth-fellowship programs founder. Even a very average youth director can manage wonders if, with the backing of a knowledgeable parish minister and a strong board of Christian education, he or she goes about the business in the right way.

The first step in any proper process of youth program development involves identifying the things that the program seeks to accomplish. In brief, the appointed task is to accomplish significant work in a handful of growth areas where all young people need to progress if they are to mature into responsible, confident, socially adequate Christian adults. Much invaluable information, partially Christian and partially secular, is available to guide the board of Christian education and the parish minister in their selection of the youth fellowship's program goals. Twenty years of experience in this area lead me to suggest these: (1) Christian character development, (2) Christian interpersonal relationships, (3) Christian family relationships, (4) Christian faith development, (5) Christian social issues, (6) Christian service opportunities, and (7) Christian work identity development.

An exhaustive discussion of the program possibilities under each of these goals is beyond the scope of this chapter, but a brief comment on each will suggest the potential. Christian character development covers all questions of personal ethics, attitudes, and personal conduct. Christian interpersonal relationships have to do with the young Christian's interaction with peers, classmates, neighbors, and the associated problems. Goals in the area of Christian family relationships engage those knotty adolescent problems with parents, brothers, and sisters. Christian faith development provides nonclassroom experiential opportunities for young Christians to develop personal commitment to Jesus Christ and his church (as through retreats, "lock-ins," et cetera). Christian social issues introduce the Christian young person to the host of unresolved injustices, deprivations, and tragedies that blight the lives of so many in the modern world. Christian service opportunities afford young Christians a direct opportunity to work in the Christian mission (as, for example, by participating in a study-work project in Appalachia or at a South Dakota Indian mission station). Christian work identity development closes with what Erik Erikson insists is the adolescent's chief problem. I must make personal comment here.

Erikson writes in one of his most important monographs, "It is primarily the inability to settle on an occupational identity which disturbs young people."[2] That being so, the failure of the home, the school, and the parish church to assist the adolescent's quest for a vocation is an unforgivable oversight. For example, how many fathers have ever taken their sons and daughters to their place of business so they might observe their activities over an entire workday? Or again, how many high schools include opportunities to learn about and observe bonafide members of the American working force—factory workers, business executives, physicians, teachers, clergymen, et cetera—as part of their regular course of studies? Or finally, how many adults, of whatever kind or in whatever role, have ever made it clear that the work identity of a young person between the ages of six and at least sixteen is that of a student? These are oversights that the youth program in the American parish church is admirably equipped to correct. In the light of the terrible tribulations American adolescents suffered through in the 1960s, mostly because of a radical identity crisis, it is negligent of America's adults—and particularly its Christian adults—not to promptly undertake the remedies at hand.

So much for goals. Preparing program schedules for the junior and senior youth fellowships is the next order of business. At both levels—the junior youth fellowship, which includes young people prior to confirmation, and the senior youth fellowship, which serves adolescents who have attained full church membership—a properly devised interest finder is the way to begin. These interest finders should be constructed with the participation of the young people concerned or their elected officers. But a very important process, which represents the implementation of the goals described above, needs to be followed.

Under each of the seven youth-fellowship program emphases, at least fifteen specific programs that constitute legitimate aspects of that concern are listed on the interest finder. Directions across the top of the page read as follows: "Choose not more than five program topics under each heading. Do not exercise all or any choices if particular programs don't interest you." Boxes along the left-hand side of the interest finder will be provided for the participants' check marks. Obviously, specific topics under each of the goal headings on the junior and senior youth fellowship interest finders will be chosen to meet the differing life situations of younger and older adolescents.

After the interest finders have been filled out by the two fellowships, usually at the first fall meeting of each group, the results will be collated. A half-year program, covering the first semester, will then be drawn up and confirmed by the youth group, out of those topics which received the greatest number of votes. The young people, before the final program is designed, should establish a commitment to doing some significant work under each of the seven goals or headings at some time during the church year. Topics listed under Christian Interpersonal Relationships may have attracted the most interest, while those under Christian Faith Development the least; but through prior understanding and commitment of the entire fellowship, at least a few of the highest rated program topics under Christian Faith Development will appear on the final youth-fellowship schedule. Thus some significant work is done on each of the youth fellowship's goals. The specific area of application within the goal is precisely where most of the young people, in that particular fellowship and in that particular year, desire most to work. And the end result will be not only a program of considerable interest to the participants because they designed it themselves, but also a balanced program, in which all the growth needs of Christian adolescents receive some serious attention at just those points where the participants feel their importance.

Adult advisers are essential. Couples of high Christian character, emotional stability, and possessing strong marriages function best. Again, more is better than less. In my experience, five couples, acting as youth advisers for each youth fellowship, have proved the optimum number. Those couples should be chosen from different age and vocational groups. Nothing is better for all concerned than to have a good mix (I once had a mechanic, a business executive, a dentist, a teacher, and a research chemist) involved with their spouses as adult advisers to the same youth fellowship.

Using multiple youth advisers provides the same advantages as a team-teaching approach to the church school. Each pair of advisers has to conduct only five youth programs during an entire church year. Therefore no one gets overworked, and a much more diverse and highly skilled body of advisers can be enlisted. The parish young people get to know a wide variety and large number of adult church members. Substitute leadership, in case of unexpected absenteeism, presents no problem, since there are four more couples who can quickly move in. The majority of young people much prefer the diversity of adult standpoints provided by ten different adults, as against the single views of the old-fashioned youth adviser or couple. The approach to and execution of programs are invariably more fresh and interesting. And finally, the parish minister and the board of Christian education are able to build a rapidly expanding pool of adult church members who have had a pleasurable, productive experience of working with adolescents.

We now have a half-year program and five couples who have agreed to act as youth advisers for each of our two youth fellowships. The next step is to convene a meeting of youth advisers for preliminary instruction in their responsibilities and for their selection of the particular programs they would most like to supervise. The point of the latter is to fit skills and interests of particular youth advisers into specific programs chosen by the young people. Obviously people will contribute most to those programs and projects in which they are genuinely interested. For the rest, as will now be described, the adult advisers can best be educated through on-the-job training by the minister or youth director who bears staff responsibility for the youth fellowships.

The program is now ready for production. Two weeks prior to the date a particular meeting will be offered, the responsible minister or youth director makes an appointment with the adult advisers asigned to supervise it, provides them with the names of three or four young people who will assist in working up the program, and then goes over a variety of resources and techniques by which the assigned topic might be implemented. The youth advisers, without the minister or youth director present, will then meet and work out the specific shape of the event. At some convenient time prior to the actual meeting, the outcome of this final planning session will be conveyed to the responsible cleric or youth director.

Different programs require varying amounts of development by the young people and youth advisers responsible. When outside speakers, films, off-site experiences, or recreational activities are scheduled, the flow of the meeting is fairly well cut and dried. At other times, the program must be built from scratch. The important matters here are to give full range to the advisers' and young people's creativity (while having alternatives available in case they come up dry); to vary the format and location of the program so as to maintain interest; and to include as many of the available parish young people as possible in the resulting activities.

On the last matter, the parish responsibility list, covering the school grades involved in the youth programs, provides the attendance target. A youth fellowship is of no earthly use to a young person who never attends. It cannot therefore be allowed to become the posession of either an exclusive clique or a group of overly shy, often immature young people who utilize it as a primary social outlet. If the program is planned by the young people served, if its quality is invariably good, if its content is exciting, and if it is scheduled at a time when most of the parish's young people are able to attend, a modest application of attendance boosters and personal invitations will turn out previous nonattenders on a regular basis in heartening numbers. But the ones who do not appear must not be ignored! The minister, youth director, and fellowship members need to make special efforts to involve them; for these young people are often those lonely, left-out, mixed-up adolescents who need most what the parish youth fellowship program offers.

Some isolated details about youth-fellowship planning and program now need to be pulled together.

If a process similar to that just described is followed, the minister or youth director will find that he or she is free at the meeting to be essentially a participant. When the forestated principles are ignored, all too often the adult advisers do little more than serve the refreshments; the young people progressively disintegrate into a bored audience; and the staff member in charge becomes the stage manager and only actor in a one-man, ever less interesting show.

Twenty years ago, every Sunday evening I conducted first a junior youth fellowship with an average of over sixty participants, followed by a senior youth fellowship with an average of fifty participants. Well before the first of these two programs was opened, my work was done. Except under extraordinary circumstances, I sat back and enjoyed an excellent program that a set of completely prepared youth advisors and a handful of the parish youth had devised and implemented themselves.

It is an excellent idea to publish each half year's youth fellowship program, with the advisers assigned and the topic described, in a compact program booklet. At midyear, a month before the end of the first semester's program, the interest finder is again consulted, the first half year's successes and shortcomings are reviewed; and, on the basis of these data, the youth fellowships or their elected officers produce and publish the second half year's schedule.

Churches that do not already own a bus ought to consider the purchase of one. All parts of the church program will benefit. Every organization in the parish is thereby provided the means to include off-site programs on its schedule of activities. Women's guilds, golden-age groups, couples clubs, and singles organizations will be particularly benefited. But beyond question, the parish youth-fellowship program will gain the most. Interested lay persons can easily be recruited to take a course of special instruction leading to a chauffeur's license (at parish expense) in order to provide a pool of volunteer bus drivers. In recent years, our senior youth fellowships have annually gone on two-week work-study tours to our denominational home mission fields. Nothing has contributed more to the young people's Christian growth or done more to sustain year-long interest in the parish youth fellowship than these marvelous early-summer experiences.

Mention ought to be made, at this point, of vacation Bible schools and summer youth camps. Bible schools are best accomplished by combinations of churches, not necessarily adjacent to one another, that will share staffing, promotion, and funding. The vacation Bible school usually aims at children below the junior high level. However, aside from the relief afforded the mothers of the children involved, its long-term value seldom seems worth the time and effort required. Christian youth camps, especially for junior and senior high students (that is, junior and senior youth fellowship members), are another matter altogether. A young person actually receives more hours of Christian training in a one-week experience at a Christian youth camp than he or she will collect, if perfect attendance is maintained, at all the weekly church-school class sessions and youth fellowship meetings over the full ten months of the school year. Besides that, the concentrated form of the experience, the superior quality of Christian youth camp leadership (usually clergy and religious educators), the opportunity to interact with other Christian young people not previously known, and the maturing experience of living away from home, all combine to make Christian youth camping a learning experience for adolescents that cannot otherwise be equaled.

Local churches should support their denominational youth camping programs by making professional staff members available as faculty members (the time thus employed not to be counted as vacation) by underwriting a part of any parish young person's tuition, by devising a scholarship system that will permit all to attend, and by promoting the idea of regular attendance at church school and youth fellowship plus a week of Christian camping each year as the basic ingredients of a junior or senior high student's Christian education.

Funding the youth fellowship program has intentionally been left until last. Money is far from everything. But an ample budget for youth fellowship programming greatly enriches the end result. Indeed, without sufficient funding, any parish's youth fellowship program will not be able to compete with the lavish entertainment available to young people almost anywhere in the secular world.

But Christian education did not begin as children's education and it must never be permitted to end there. Jesus' first students were all adults. The original practice of celebrating believers' baptism only, a practice probably taken over from the proselyte baptism of Judaism, points unambiguously to adult Christian education as the original norm. This is verified by what appears to have been the disciples' practice of actually keeping the children away from Jesus when he was engaged in his public teaching ministry (Mark 10:13).

The original teaching ministry of the parish church was indisputably an exercise in adult Christian education. Later, when families entered local communities of faith, a suitable apparatus for educating Christian children was devised. That development, which surely occurred before the canon was closed, influenced the inclusion of such narrative incidents, suggestive of Jesus' approval of a Christian teaching ministry to children, as the account of our Lord's conversations with rabbis in the Jerusalem Temple at age twelve, and the familiar remark with which the incident alluded to above ended: "Let the children come to me, do not hinder them; for to such belongs to kingdom of God" (Mark 10:14).

The important thing to tie down, then, is that adult Christian education came first, and wherever it has not retained its primacy in the church's teaching ministry, the decline of Christian education for children has followed.

The passing of the adult lay Bible student in my childhood, several of whom once could be found in anybody's local congregation, presaged the watering down of church-school curricula to the point where eventually, in many church-school classrooms, no specifically Christian education whatsoever took place. This circumstance is precisely what led a number of main-line American Protestant denominations, almost twenty years ago, to insist once more upon the overriding importance of adult Christian education; and much good came out of their concern.

As to specifics, in the period immediately following World War II, most active parish churches offered a variety of breakfast, lunchtime, week-night or (usually for women only) weekday adult Christian education opportunities. There were Bible study groups, prayer groups, Christian social action seminars, and mission study circles. The Sunday morning Bible class, of course, continued as it always had, though in many communions it was now overshadowed by these newer innovations. But then came the evening television blitzkrieg, dozens of new uses for adult free time, and the cynicism of the sixties. Weekday adult evening education, in the main-line Protestant denominations, dried up. Special breakfast and lunchtime opportunities hung on, though usually involving far fewer adults and being specifically limited to such periods as Advent and Lent. Only the evangelical and theologically conservative denominations were able to sustain the traditional teaching and adult Christian education activities of the American church. By the mid 1960s, it was therefore clear something had to be done.

Something was done. American Christian educators and parish ministers began looking seriously into the possibilities of an "extended Sunday morning." The idea was both ingenious and simple. Busy American Christians would be offered an opportunity to invest two and one half hours, instead of an hour and fifteen minutes, in their celebration of the Lord's Day. And instead of merely going to morning worship, they and their families would be treated to a quality Christian education experience as well.

Where such extended Sunday morning programs have been

properly installed and imaginatively implemented, scores of parishes have experienced substantial, if not astonishing, increases in Sunday morning congregations, as well as revitalization of their entire life. Those enjoying such happy results report that the important keys to success are: (1) offer educational programs and related activities for all ages in that part of the two and one half hour period not devoted to morning worship; (2) concentrate the parish's major adult Christian education opportunities in this period; and (3) design a complete experience, involving worship and Christian education that the entire family can begin and end together.

By way of expanding and illustrating these concepts, I shall conclude this chapter by describing the extended Sunday morning program used by the particular parish church I currently serve.

Our church educational emphasis opens at 9:15 on every Sunday morning of the school year. A single service of public worship, running from 10:30 to 11:30, concludes it. Coffee, juice, and sweet rolls are available in the church parlor for the first hour. Only coffee is available after the service. By ending morning worship at 11:30, we afford an opportunity for members to enjoy fellowship after the service without feeling they must rush home and take the Sunday dinner out of the oven. The half hour between 11:30 and noon also offers an opportunity for parish boards and committees to conduct brief emergency meetings, which otherwise would necessitate a special trip downtown to church on a week-night.

From 9:15 to 10:15, the following programs are offered: children's choir rehearsal, bell choir rehearsal, extended-time activities (essentially a program of short trips, church-related handwork, and mission projects for young children), our confirmation department classes for eighth and ninth graders (involving a two-year required curriculum in preparation for church membership, and taught by the associate minister), the adult seminar, and the adult lecture. The last pair of endeavors deserve further elaboration.

There are two formats that adults like for Christian education. One is a seminar, where each can contribute directly and continually to the process. The other is a lecture, with a formal presentation followed by a question-and-answer period. We provide both, scheduling them against each other, at 9:15. The adult seminar is conducted in a medium-sized room, around rectangular tables that have been pushed together so that seminar members are essentially seated in a circle, with plenty of available tabletop for their papers, textbooks, and coffee cups. The adult lecture is held in the church chapel. Those attending sit in row pews, with the resource person speaking from the lectern or pulpit.

Interest finders are devised, one for the adult seminar and another for the adult lecture. The adult seminar interest finder contains approximately ten topics under each of three general headings: Family Relations and Personal Issues, Social Themes, and General Issues. The adult lecture interest finder is also broken down under three general headings—Bible and Church History, Personal and Pastoral Issues, and General—with ten options likewise listed under each. These instruments are made available to the parish for just two weeks in early May. The directions under their titles ask that only those adults who are interested in attending one or more of these offerings fill out an interest finder, and that not more than ten of the thirty listed program selections be checked. The interest finders for both the adult seminar and the adult lecture are then collected and totaled, and an annual schedule for each is devised from those programs which received the most votes.

Finally, the staff checks the end result to make certain that different sorts of programs will be offered at such a time as to engage the widest spread of adult interest. For example, we would not offer "Grief, Tragedy, and Death" in the adult seminar over the same three-week period we were presenting "Middle-Age Life Crises" in the adult lecture; whereas we might very well simultaneously schedule an adult seminar on "World Poverty" against an adult lecture on "The World of the Prophets." Final schedules are approved by the board of Christian education in the late spring, and the summer is used for preparation.

Some further thoughts arise out of many years' experience with adult seminars and lectures. Particular offerings ought never to be more than five presentations in duration. Three or four sessions are better. The old idea of simply having "an adult seminar" or "an adult Bible class" soon limits participation to a small clique. People are unwilling to begin something that goes on forever, and they are embarrassed by dropping out—especially if their friends are in the group or an admired teacher or minister is the resource person. By setting up the adult seminar and adult lecture in brief three-to five-week offerings, greater variety is possible and participants can commit themselves to a limited short-range obligation that will complete a total learning experience. Thus many times the number who would have participated under the old system become actively involved.

At the present moment, our adult seminar and adult lecture programs both possess a core of participants who are invariably present; and these are augmented with an ever-fluctuating body of others, who at times have filled the program areas to overflowing when the topic has been of particular interest. Attendance at both programs has increased each year, and we have seen a healthy transfer of adults back and forth between the seminar and lecture as programs of special interest have been presented.

Most parish churches possess an untapped wealth of competent lay persons who are experts in specific areas. We have been able to find leadership for all but a very few of our adult seminars in our own membership. The occasional program for which no qualified resource leader exists in our parish is led by a specialist brought in from the wider community, his or her honorarium being covered by a modest adult education budget. It has been my personal practice, for the last eighteen years, to offer the adult lecture myself. This obligation provides me with an opportunity to exercise my teaching ministry in ways that are not possible through the sermon; many exciting relationships between material presented in the adult lecture and that offered from the pulpit have been possible; and the necessity of preparing the adult lectures during the summer months has proved an excellent discipline and opportunity for continuing professional education.

The 10:30 to 11:30 hour on Sunday mornings during the school year contains just two things—classroom sessions for the lower divisions of the church school (nursery through seventh grade) and Lord's Day worship for all the rest of the parish. Nursery through seventh grades attend Family Sundays approximately nine times during the school year. The occasions selected are either festal Sundays, such as Thanksgiving and Christmas, or Sundays where something of special interest, like baptism or confirmation, will take place. These are also the only Sundays on which our children's choirs perform. Our youngest children remain in the service for approximately the first fifteen minutes, during which the hymns, prayers, and responses appearing in the order of worship involve materials utilized in the youngsters' own church school programs. We feel it is important for even very small children to become familiar, in a positive way, with adult Sunday morning worship. However, Family Sundays reduce the all too brief church school classroom teaching session by at least twenty minutes. Therefore some compromise such as that just described is in order. Unfortunately too many parish churches still have the children in church every Sunday—quite often, it would seem, simply to encourage their parents' attendance and to entertain the old folks.

Assuming the team teaching approach outlined earlier, all church school faculty members should be able to attend the regular Sunday worship services of the congregation at least half of the time; and the confirmation class, having its weekly exercise at the earlier hour, is free and expected to attend morning worship as well.

So I have outlined a modern comprehensive Christian teaching ministry, involving all members and ages, that could be installed in pratically any parish church. Many of the older Christian educational forms and habits have been modified or discarded, principally in the interest of concentrating as many Christian education opportunities as possible in an extended Sunday morning experience involving the entire family. The increasing busyness of most American Christians, the recreational alternatives to religious pursuits, and the ever lengthening roadways between the newest residential divisions and the downtown churches dictate a move toward concentration, quality programs, and simultaneous worship and educational opportunities for the entire family by today's parish churches.

I close this chapter on the teaching ministry of the parish church with still another and final word of the Lord, which not only spells out our immense obligation to provide Christian education for all ages but also admirably summarizes the particular process just elaborated:

> And Jesus came and said to [his disciples], "All authority in heaven and on earth has been given to me. Go therefore and make disciples of all nations, baptizing them in the name of the Father and of the Son and of the Holy Spirit, teaching them to observe all that I have commanded you." (Matt. 28:18-20)

The parish church that competently and faithfully fulfills this sacred charge will not only flourish but may also depend upon being the beneficiary of our Lord's most comforting promise, rendered on that same occasion: "And lo, I am with you always, to the close of the age."

The Pastoral Care of a Parish

Anything a minister does for a parishioner involves pastoral care. Carroll Wise's definition measures a more restricted understanding and shapes the following discussion. A distinguished professor of pastoral psychology and counseling, Dr. Wise writes: "Pastoral care is the art of communicating the inner-meaning of the Gospel to persons at the point of their need."[1]

A pair of creative restrictions proceed from this definition. To begin with, even though the practice of pastoral care may be primarily concerned with loving, forgiving, and reconciling, the prophetic demands for justice, righteousness, and obedience to the Law need to inform the process as well. Obviously this condition lays restraints on the clergyman as pastoral counselor; for even when a parish minister is dealing with some despairing skeptic who desperately needs to believe that "God is love," he can never legitimately ignore "What does the Lord require of you . . . ?" (Mic. 6:8). The other restriction arises from the fact that neither in theory nor in practice can the parish minister as pastoral counselor control his or her clientele. All persons seeking help, regardless of who they are or what their needs may be, must be accepted as counselees. These conditions dictate the therapeutic process appropriate to the pastoral care of a parish. They also identify the essential office parish ministers occupy within the local health-care community. I shall expand these observations later in this chapter. Let us now turn to a consideration of the ingredients essential to the process itself.

Foremost is the parish minister. To be an effective Christian pastoral counselor, a minister needs to possess certain technical skills, a clear grasp of his or her role, and considerable personal strength. As to professional training, he or she should have taken three or four seminary-level courses in pastoral care and a short-term internship, under professional supervision, in a medical or psychiatric facility. Many theological schools now require at least this much training of anyone seeking the B.D. or M.Div. degrees. Equivalent courses and clinical experiences are widely available to clerics who may have missed them. And after graduation, since this instruction provides only a basic foundation, parish ministers need to avail themselves of continuing educational opportunities in order to keep their pastoral counseling skills current.

Beyond adequate training, the parish minister as pastoral counselor must be an emotionally stable individual. Parishioners to whom they must relate in other ways often project destructive or self-destructive feelings upon their pastoral counselor. The emotional content of a serious personal or interpersonal disorder can be overwhelming. Fantasies and exploitation are common. Frequently, parish ministers are consulted after other therapists have been refused or have failed. All too often, in the tradition of cleansing lepers, causing the blind to see, and restoring the insane to their right minds, they are expected to work miracles on the order of Jesus. And, depending upon the issue, the parish minister may either be exalted to the right hand of God or condemned as an uncaring fake.

But a serious calling of God and his Christ is alone what makes the pastoral care of a parish possible. Without such a vocational sense, no parish minister can offer effective pastoral care to the parish and community. For an authentic Christian pastoral ministry is too difficult, too time-consuming, and often too painful for any minister to accomplish properly on his or her own strength alone. Earlier comments on the parish minister's professional devotional life take on their deepest meanings here. The parish minister who attempts to pursue a serious pastoral ministry without proper attention to his or her private devotional life will very soon dry up or lose the Christian foundations of the pastoral role altogether.

A final historical footnote on the parish minister as pastoral counselor is worth mentioning. Just twenty-two years ago, Liston Pope, then dean of the Yale Divinity School, "predicted that pastoral counseling would pass off the scene because it was a fad."[2] No reputable Christian seminary would support that opinion today. But nevertheless this unfortunate view persists. Indeed, Dr. Pope's observation reveals why many older clerics show little interest in a professional pastoral ministry, as well as why such a large number of parish ministers of all ages—because of their training and inclination—still do not offer a modern pastoral counseling ministry. More will be said about this later.

The setting in which pastoral counseling is conducted constitutes a second major ingredient of the process. A warm and relaxing atmosphere, where the pastoral counselor and counselee may sit in comfortable chairs at a table in a large, softly lighted room, has definite advantages. The counseling area must be soundproof. Its doors ought to be watched by an office secretary stationed outside to prevent interruptions. And the counseling facility needs to be located in a place immediately accessible to the parish and the community.

Until very recently, all parish minsters based their pastoral activities on an ancient "rural" model of ministry, which was at least a thousand years old when Oliver Goldsmith (1728–74) rhapsodized about it in his famous poem "The Village Preacher." Here the parish minister's study is in the parsonage. The church remains tightly locked between Sundays, unless a specific activity is scheduled. The clergy keep no specific office hours. Such counseling as may be done occurs either in the parsonage or at the counselee's home. The substance of this pastoral ministry is moral admonition, scripture, prayer, and/or large amounts of common sense. Not infrequently, these exercises are still referred to as conferences. Quite apart from the concept and content that shape the rural model of parish ministry, it is almost impossible to conduct any sort of modern pastoral counseling in such a setting.

The senior minister's study in my present parish was specifically designed to facilitate pastoral care. The room is of a good size, decorated in soft gold colors. The desk is off in one corner. A round table, surrounded by four leather armchairs, fills most of the floor space. The lighting is warm and indirect. Tea and coffee are available. The overall effect soon puts most people at ease, and the parish minister is presented as a friend and equal, rather than as another authority figure glowering across a desk.

A third essential ingredient of effective pastoral counseling is the parish minister's keeping of regular office hours. Many of the most important and productive helping opportunities are initiated by impulse. Someone with a problem drives by the church, sees the minister's automobile in its assigned parking spot, pulls into the church parking lot, and asks the secretary if the minister is free. So another needy soul finds access to the love of Christ and the local health-care community.

But if regular hours and an accessible office with a sensitive secretary out front maximize opportunities for effective pastoral ministry, the vulnerability of the parish minister because of these practices is surely maximized as well. There are so many other things besides pastoral counseling that demand his or her attention. A sermon must be written, hospitals visited, and a host of administrative matters addressed. A few parishioners, with time to waste, see no reason why they should not regularly be entertained by the minister. An even larger number, knowing their parish minister is in the office, become incensed when they are not permitted entrée at once. But only parish ministers without active pastoral ministries can keep open office doors. When control at this point is lost, a minister can be of no pastoral counseling usefulness to anyone at all. Some parish ministers maintain a second, hideaway study for use at times when they simply must not be disturbed. Others meet such emergencies by working at the parsonage. Unfortunately, a still larger group have resolved this dilemma by refusing to keep regular office hours.

One further reference needs to be made to Oliver Goldsmith's village preacher and that ancient rural model of pastoral ministry, here respecting general access to the parish minister. In an earlier day, parish ministers were instilled with a holy obligation to call, at least once each year, on every home in the parish. As recently as two decades ago, the most conscientious parish ministers of my acquaintance maintained such a practice, even publishing in their weekly bulletins the streets they expected to be calling in on each day of the coming week. Such approaches have long since been abandoned by knowledgeable pastoral counselors. But unhappily, many parishioners still expect their parish minister to make an annual call. Any cleric who spends most of his or her counseling time visiting untroubled Christians who are already staunch church members is thereby rendered completely unavailable to just those individuals who need help most. On this head, both parish ministers and their parishioners would do well to remember Jesus' rejoinder to those scribes and Pharisees who criticized him for spending all his time with prostitutes, tax collectors, and other sinners, instead of calling on the "good people." As reported in the Third Gospel, Jesus said, "Those who are well have no need of a physician, but those who are sick" (Luke 5:31-32).

A fourth essential ingredient of the pastoral counseling process is the pastoral seal. Pastoral care of a parish is impossible without it. For neither God nor the people will long abide a minister who does not keep confidences. As a formal pledge, the pastoral seal is a sacred commitment, publicly offered at the time of ordination and renewed at each subsequent service of installation. In substance, it is a solemn vow that the parish minister will not divulge any information that a counselee desires to keep confidential. Occasionally, information needs to be shared with some other professional (i.e., a psychiatrist, internist, lawyer). But this step ought to be taken only with great circumspection, on the basis of the other professional's need to know, and always with the consent of the counselee. Ministers who cannot or will not keep the pastoral seal are failures as pastoral counselors. In time, their indiscretions become common knowledge, and those most in need of their services will go elsewhere.

Some years ago, a competent parish minister, following a questionable practice then much in vogue, brought several recent counseling experiences into a series of Sunday sermons. Names were not mentioned. Specifics were so disguised that actual events could not be surmised. Nevertheless, that sermon series ruined the clergyman's usefulness to his parish. Present and past counselees recognized their particular troubles. Prospective counselees concluded that, should they seek help from the parish minister, their predicament would end up in some future sermon. It mattered not that the preacher had thoroughly disguised his illustrations. In the minds of the majority of his parishioners, he had broken the pastoral seal and so could no longer be trusted with their most intimate concerns. A chastened but much wiser parish minister soon thereafter accepted a new charge. And he has not brought his pastoral counseling ministry into the pulpit since.

Before we turn to a description of the various pastoral-care ministries modern parish churches offer, some comments on a serious misunderstanding are in order.

The size of a particular church's pastoral care ministry is primarily determined by two factors—how available this ministry is, and how effective it is deemed to be. There are parish churches located in hellholes of human misery whose ministers will honestly tell you they receive few calls for pastoral care. Other parish ministers, serving supposedly low-problem constituencies, confess to being overwhelmed by the demands for pastoral care their parishes and communities lay upon them. Clearly, the difference between these situations lies in how prospective clients view the quality and availability of the services offered. If the minister seems uninterested, is usually unavailable, or has not proved of much use to people in trouble, his or her services will not be in high demand. If he or she is always interested, available, and has helped many, people will come from miles around to avail themselves of counseling. Jesus, and later his disciples, were constantly mobbed by those seeking pastoral care. At least once, a hole was broken through the roof of a house where Jesus was teaching, to admit the sick (Mark 2:4). Tormented souls cried out after him and sought to touch him in crowds (Matt. 9:21; Mark 7:26). And at least in one instance, people lined the public highway with their invalids, in hopes that the shadow of the apostles might fall on them and heal them as they passed by (Acts 5:15).

Only the scribes and Pharisees denigrated the earliest Christians' pastoral ministry. They complained about healing on the Sabbath and suggested that Jesus worked his wonders through the powers of Beelzebul (Mark 3:2; Matt. 12:24). But their carping was never so much a matter of outraged piety as it was of jealousy over the unfavorable comparison common people had rendered between Jesus' ministry of pastoral care and theirs.

Five distinct types of professional ministry include most of what pastoral care in the parish church involves—instructional care, hospital care, shut-in care, bereavement care, and crisis care.

Instructional care properly focuses upon the major Christian life events—baptism, confirmation, marriage. In each case, specific instruction should precede the celebration of the sacrament or office. It is an excellent practice to augment formal counseling sessions with outside reading of pertinent materials provided free of cost by the parish.

If infant baptism is to be celebrated, the parents should be required to attend at least one prebaptismal counseling session. (Usually this will be a group counseling experience involving the parents of all babies to be baptized at a particular service.) The meaning of the sacrament is there explained, the obligations of the parents and the church for the future Christian nurture of the child are reviewed, and the service itself is described. Where adults are to be baptized, confirmation is always also involved. Hence a careful course of study on Christian doctrine and the meaning of church membership, supervised by the minister, should precede the rite.

Confirmation, will usually, however, involve baptized Christians, twelve to fourteen years old, who have recently completed extensive preparation for church membership. Our present confirmation curriculum consists of two years in the parish church school's confirmation department (eighth and ninth grades), which is taught by our associate minister, and a final, nine-weeks "pastor's class," immediately preceding confirmation, taught by the senior minister. A recent study conducted by the United Church of Christ reveals that far too little confirmation education is taking place in most American churches today. Past and present failures at this point contribute substantially to the large number of uninformed, uncommitted, uninterested adults currently registered on the rolls of America's churches.[3]

Marriage counseling, or more properly premarital counseling, should precede any celebration of holy matrimony conducted in a Christian church. At the very least, a multiple-session process needs to be undertaken in which the financial, sexual, interpersonal, family, and religious aspects of marriage are reviewed and discussed. If problems materialize, the premarital counseling process should be expanded with additional sessions. The best procedure is to halt the process at the point problems arise; insert additional counseling sessions directed to resolving the specific trouble; and, after the issue has been resolved, go on with the general counseling. Obviously, such a procedure necessitates scheduling the first premarital counseling session at least three months before the marriage is to be celebrated. Last-minute counseling leaves no room for unexpected problems. As part of every premarital counseling process, the bride should be referred to a qualified gynecologist for a premarital physical examination. When serious problems arise, the parish minister ought immediately to divert the premarital counseling into referral counseling; and if possible, plans for the marriage should be temporarily postponed until a competent psychiatrist or clinical psychologist returns the prospective bride and groom to the pastoral care of the parish minister. Appropriate counseling for second marriages is extremely important and should never be neglected.

Hospital care offers unique pastoral opportunities to the parish minister. But health-care institutions have activity patterns and policies that need to be learned. Therefore, upon taking up a new charge, ministers are well advised to seek out the hospital chaplain, adminstrator, or some interested physician, from whom they may learn such things as the most convenient visiting hours; the hospital's policies governing the clergy; the locations of the emergency service, the intensive care unit, and the family surgical waiting room; and the names of hospital staff personnel to whom parish ministers may apply for additional information or help.

Here follows a specific list of dos and don'ts pertaining to hospital care:

1. Hospital visits ought to be made on stated days of each week, except when emergencies require immediate or continuous attention.

2. Anyone staying in a local hospital should be visited not less than twice a week. Where a multiple ministerial staff exists, hospital calling should involve all who have pastoral responsibilities, and the incidence of calls should be increased to three or four times a week.

3. The assistance of nearby ministers should be solicited when parishioners are hospitalized out of town or when, for any reason, the minister is unable to provide personal attention.

4. Records should be kept of all visits, indicating the patient's condition, any noteworthy observations, and what the minister did while there (e.g., offered prayer, left devotional literature, agreed to call on a family member). Such records, maintained in the church office, are indispensable when more than a single minister is covering hospital work. Upon the patient's release from the hospital, his or her record card should be moved from an active status file, under the hospital's name, to an alphabetized inactive file. Such a procedure enables the parish minister to discover immediately the medical past history of a parishioner if rehospitalization occurs.

5. If they are not well themselves or if they have some

potentially contagious condition such as a cold, ministers should never visit hospitals except in times of dire emergency.

6. Where a patient is found to be particularly anxious or dangerously ill, it is an excellent idea for the minister to leave a calling card with the charge nurse, so that he or she can be immediately reached if pastoral attention is needed.

7. Respecting visiting technique, the most important rules for effective hospital care are: listen as closely as possible to the needs of the patient; deal with the patient's agenda; do not be falsely optimistic about the patient's condition, for counterfeit support, once recognized, will increase the patient's anxiety and feeling of isolation; do not be the voice of doom in an effort to precipitate religious fervor, for such tactics are exploitative and often produce anger or despair; be at ease in the patient's presence; be guided by the patient's desires (sometimes these will have to be guessed) as to whether or not you pray, read scripture, or serve communion; and, above all, neither run in and run out nor stay too long.

8. The attending physician, not the parish minister, should inform the patient and the family of the medical prognosis. The minister often afterward plays an essential role in helping both to cope with the verdict.

9. A minister ought never to do anything, in ministry to a particular hospital patient, that the attending physician has indicated should not be done.

10. An ordained cleric must be available to the parish for emergency hospital care and crisis counseling, 24 hours a day, 365 days a year.

11. If a minister cannot comfortably function as a pastor in the presence of sick or dying persons, professional help should be secured at once. It is nothing to be ashamed of. Young physicians frequently have the same problem. Short-term counseling, or even a simple airing of one's anxieties with a trusted colleague, often works wonders. In years past, two young ministers just out of seminary came to me with this trouble. For the next several months, we made all our hospital calls together. Within that period and without further help, their irrational anxieties disappeared. No one but the two of us knew what we were about. But had these young men not

had the courage to talk to someone about their true feelings, this vulnerability could very well have ruined a pastorate or even driven them from the parish ministry.

Shut-in care is often a neglected responsibility. Many parish ministers who call faithfully in local hospitals do not provide regular shut-in care for homebound and institutionalized parishioners. The two keys to responsible shut-in care are semiannual personal calls by the parish minister on each homebound or institutionalized parishioner, and continuing care by an active board of deacons and deaconesses, which the minister will directly supervise. It has long been my practice to call on all parish shut-ins during Advent and again during Lent. These visitations are announced in the church bulletin. The entire parish shut-in list is published at the same time, together with an urging that parishioners remember homebound members in their prayers, with cards, and with visits. During my own Advent and Lenten calls, I carefully note the condition, surroundings, and needs of each shut-in. Besides serving communion, if such is requested, I ask if there are any other ways in which the church might be helpful. These findings go into a confidential report, which becomes a part of the church's permanent pastoral care file and is shared with the board of deacons and deaconesses on the basis of need to know.

Between my Advent and Lenten calls, members of the board of deacons and deaconesses, augmented by a selected group of parishioners who enjoy and function well in this ministry, cover the entire parish shut-in list. A subcommittee of the board of deacons and deaconesses coordinates the effort, making certain each shut-in receives the attention and personal support that will prove most beneficial. These few thoughts on conducting a parish shut-in ministry may be worth setting down:

1. We assign a particular parishioner, congenial to the shut-in, to conduct weekly, semiweekly, or monthly visits on a long-term basis. Other church members may also drop in and usually do. But the primary responsibility remains with the individual designated by the board of deacons and deaconesses as the permanent visitor. A real relationship thereby

develops, and changes in the shut-in's circumstances are much more quickly noted and reported to the minister.

2. Every shut-in is offered a Bible, a church hymnal, a copy of the church bulletin, a list of all religious broadcasts (and if needed, an inexpensive radio), subscriptions to newspapers or magazines that interest him or her, and hobby materials. Birthdays, anniversaries, Christmas, and Easter are remembered with a card or gift. Following ancient practice, rooted in the daily common meal of the earliest Christian church, we receive a free-will deacon and deaconess offering at each celebration of Holy Communion, to be used only "for the relief and need of those in our parish." The monies so collected have more than covered all expenditures involved in our shut-in ministry.

3. Our shut-in care is built around a weekly broadcast of our Sunday morning worship service. More will be said about the value of a radio ministry in the chapter on stewardship and evangelism. Within the present context, it ought to be noted that we design the service with our shut-in members in mind. They are greeted in the announcement period and specifically referred to in the pastoral prayer. Our purpose is to make them participants in, rather than merely listeners to, the public worship of the parish. Providing our shut-in members with Bibles, church hymnals, and the church bulletin (which always contains the order of worship and is delivered on Friday) serves the same end.

4. Nothing does more to improve shut-in care than a parish minister or part-time lay parish caller to provide direct staff support for the shut-in ministry. We currently employ an excellent part-time lay parish caller.

Bereavement care begins with notification of a parishioner's terminal illness or death. It may actually start a year or more before the funeral. It always continues for sometime afterward. And the process essentially involves either helping the next of kin work through the death of a significant member of their family, or assisting a terminally ill person, who grieves over his own approaching death, to "die well" (a phrase coined by Elisabeth Kübler-Ross). Dr. Kübler-Ross' major work, *On Death and Dying,*[4] offers the finest statement currently in print of the task that the parish minister needs to accomplish. Space limitations do not permit a detailed rehearsal of that discussion here; but, in substance, Dr. Kübler-Ross argues that we know a great deal about the process of bereavement; both the terminally ill individual and his or her family members go through identical bereavement feelings; acceptance and peace are attained only after sufficient "grief work" has been accomplished; and properly trained doctors, ministers, and other helping professionals are capable of immeasurably facilitating good results. The minister should, if possible, establish a solid relationship with the family before the terminally ill person dies. He or she should not hesitate to seek help and medical support from the family's physician during periods when the next of kin's bereavement trauma is most severe. He or she will contact the family daily, in the period between death and the funeral, using the first of these opportunities to work out the funeral service in consultation with the undertaker the family has chosen. After the funeral, the minister will maintain unobtrusive contact with the survivors until certain all are capable of carrying on without further pastoral support. Such care not infrequently involves pastoral surveillance for a period of eighteen months to two years. But as soon as the survivors are able and willing to stand on their own feet, the minister should withdraw. Bereavement is a negotiation by which an individual withdraws his or her emotional capital from a now deceased person for the purpose of investing it in new and significant others. Bereavement care and the minister's special responsibility therefore end whenever these transactions are completed. Both for the minister's and the parishioner's sakes, the minister must not continue an unnecessary supportive role beyond that point.

Crisis care is what most Christians think about when the subject of pastoral counseling arises. In active pastoral ministries, this kind of caring usually demands more time of the parish minister than any of the other four. A bewildering complex of tragedy and trouble falls under this office. Family problems, marriage problems, anxiety, depression, anger, jealousy, and moral breakdown follow one another in dizzy array. Needless to say, it is impossible to generalize about approach or technique. It is even more unlikely that any parish minister can master the necessary therapeutic skills to handle all these varities of woe. The minister therefore must amass a solid background of general pastoral skills and experience, a comprehensive acquaintance with local health-care agencies and professionals, and the ability to make general diagnoses of presented problems. But the single most important thing is that he or she be trained in and utilize referral counseling as the backbone of his or her crisis care. With some extended comment on that proposition, this chapter on the pastoral care of a parish church will close.

More harm than the mind can imagine has been done by well-intentioned parish ministers who refuse to refer distressed community members and parishioners. In earlier days, when psychiatry and religion were at swords' points, this tragedy was touted as a virtue; and the parish minister, much to the despair of the medical profession, attacked substantial physical, emotional, and social malfunctions—solely on his own—with moral admonitions, the Bible, and prayer. More recently, seminaries have seriously involved themselves and their students in secular healing techniques, and the dividing wall of hostility between theology and psychiatry has, for the most part, been torn down. But this happy development has in turn been compromised by overambitious parish ministers. Partially mastered nondirective counseling techniques, sensitivity training, and transactional analysis are currently being applied, in the name of pastoral ministry, to parishioners and community members with serious psychosomatic disorders. Such so-called modern pastoral counseling ministries are, of course, every bit as dangerous to the counselee as were yesterday's Christian assaults on the devil. The following three principles of limitation should therefore govern all proper pastoral care in any parish church:

1. *Limitations of time.* Recent studies indicate that in our country approximately 50 percent of all healing opportunities originate in some minister's office. When one considers all the coronaries, internal medical problems, broken legs, and automobile accidents that originate elsewhere, this is a

remarkable statistic. Such activity levels also indicate that any parish minister who will not refer either does not have a very active pastoral ministry or is not giving adequate care to most of those who seek help. For example, working with one serious marriage problem on a continuing basis requires at least two hours of direct counseling a week, for a period that might last several years, as well as another hour of desk work on the preparation of a proper case record. Ministers who enter into this kind of long-term counseling relationship thereby restrict their usefulness to no more than three or four situations at any one time. But since the minister cannot limit the number of clients seeking help, he or she is soon forced to accept much more direct counseling than can possibly be handled. This road eventually dead-ends in poor sermons, inadequate parish administration, steadily diminishing community involvement, an unhappy home life, and finally a parish minister who is of no use to anyone. Each year, many very fine clerics leave the parish church because they no longer can stand the self-impossed pressures entailed in a direct nonreferral pastoral-counseling ministry.

My present counseling ministry to a sizable urban parish occupies an average of twenty hours out of a seventy-hour work week. Anyone who seeks my pastoral care receives full and thorough professional attention. But my responsibilities are fulfilled only because the largest number of situations (and all that would require lengthy therapy), after an average of two or three sessions, are referred to an appropriate health-care professional or agency.

2. *Limitations of expertise.* In the nature of things, a parish minister as pastoral counselor is a generalist. Seminary instruction, except at the advanced graduate level, does not supply sufficient training in applied skills to prepare the minister to deal with serious kinds of psychological or social disorders. Most responsible theological school education begins with the establishment of what the parish minister as pastoral counselor must not attempt to do. From here it proceeds to supply the knowledge and technique necessary to identify broad general varieties of disorder, to help and heal those conditions which are within the minister's personal

competence, and then to provide extensive training in referral counseling. On the latter head, health-care professionals have long known that the quality of a referral often determines the results secured from the therapy itself. This is to say, if a husband with an alcohol problem is driven to a psychiatrist by the threats of his wife and a judgmental minister, the professional counselor may end up dealing with a hostile, completely uncooperative patient. But if proper referral counseling sends that same alcoholic husband to the psychiatrist in a hopeful, positive frame of mind, the chance for constructive therapy is immensely improved.

But by far the most serious professional errors occur when parish ministers insist upon treating schizophrenics with transactional analysis, stomach pains of undertermined origin by the laying on of hands, and marriage problems solely with prayer. Only what is absolutely within the pastoral competence and training of a particular minister ought to receive his or her personal attention. The parish minister is but one member of a large and varied group of health-care professionals, each with unique skills and appropriate areas of therapy. Upon assuming a new pastorate, one of the first things a minister ought to do is become acquainted with the local health-care community. One excellent way of accomplishing this is by setting up interviews with church members who are physicians, lawyers, psychiatrists, and social workers. Their extensive acquaintance with what is available and its quality, as well as their special interest in their own minister's needs, usually result in immediate introductions to the professionals and services one's pastoral ministry requires.

Some individual therapists—particularly psychiatrists, surgeons, and doctors of internal medicine—persist in treating clerics as inferiors, nuisances, or worse. Those active in a minister's own parish are not likely to do so and, in my experience, have forewarned me where and with whom such attitudes might arise. But parish ministers are not entirely innocent victims. A handful have brought this unhappiness upon themselves, as well as upon the rest of us, by impeding the proper functions of other professionals in the healing community. In any event, the best way to raise a right appreciation of the parish minister's professional worth, as a member of the local health-care community, is through a competent referral ministry and the properly limited exercise of Christian pastoral care.

3. *Limitations of relationship.* The most compelling reason for prompt referral of persons with serious psychological or social disorders is that keeping them would fundamentally change the relationship between the parishioner and his or her minister. When the minister becomes deeply involved in a parishioner's troubles, he or she often comes into possession of terribly personal and sensitive information. Later, after the pastoral counseling is over, both pastor and counselee try and return to their former relationship as though the recent crisis had never occurred. But this is frequently impossible. The parishioner harbors anxieties and resentments over the fact that the parish minister knows something he or she desperately wishes the minister did not. The minister is likewise inhibited by past knowledge in future dealings with the former counselee. General statements, teaching, and sermons are sometimes received as private communications between the parish minister and former counselees. There is also the likelihood that the parishioner, having come to enjoy the counseling relationship, will not permit the minister to terminate it, even when all need for such a ministry is past. Once more, the inability of the minister to limit or control his or her clientele is decisively present. The minister who does not refer, sooner or later either becomes trapped into continuing a counseling relationship that has become a definite obstacle to further healing or is faced with summarily terminating a counseling relationship at the risk of permanently alienating the parishioner.

Parish ministers must never forget that they are many things to each member of their church—preacher, pastor, teacher, administrator, friend. The unique advantages of their generalist role should never be carelessly squandered. There are times when every parish minister must venture into deep waters with a parishioner because the individual will not accept any other therapist. But capitulation under these circumstances should always be a last resort and undertaken only when the potential for good outweighs the serious side effects likely to ensue. On several occasions over the last two decades, parishioners who insisted I not refer but counsel serious problems, later, and with my support, transferred to another local parish in order to reestablish a nontherapeutic relationship with a parish minister. Here, as nowhere else, the utimate argument for concentrating on a referral pastoral counseling ministry appears.

One final word. "Pastor" comes from a Latin term that is customarily translated "shepherd." The Christian pastoral ministry is therefore a shepherding ministry, which parish ministers solemnly swear to fulfill, at the time of their ordination and at each subsequent service of installation. The most important license for this undertaking is Jesus Christ's threefold charge to Simon Peter: "Feed my lambs. . . . Tend my sheep. . . . Feed my sheep" (John 21:15-17). No parish minister who can look back on a pastorate and honestly claim to have done his or her very best with these tasks will ever have failed either the calling as a Christian pastor—or the Lord.

Stewardship and Evangelism

Stewardship and evangelism, in the American church have long rested upon questionable assumptions. Contrary to what most had believed, time, talent, and treasure have not, in recent times or in significant amounts, been withheld from the local congregation, denominational hierarchies, or theological seminaries because of dissatisfaction with public stands taken on social issues. Neither has reactionary fundamentalism proved the route to larger congregations and budgets. Rather, changing parish church membership and stewardship patterns have been influenced far more, on the one hand, by "localism," which actually testifies to the success of denominations in transmiting their concern that congregations engage in vital Christian mission where they "live and work and play"; and, on the other, by failure to stress adequately, on all levels of the American church (but particularly in its liberal parts), the main business of any parish church—namely, promoting Christian stewardship and evangelism.

These are the issues dealt with in this chapter. Christian stewardship will be addressed first. Christian evangelism will follow.

Principles of Christian Stewardship

The origins of Christian stewardship are rooted in the foundation statements on biblical anthropology published in the first and second chapters of Genesis, where we read: "And God said to them [the male and female], '. . . have dominion over the fish of the sea and over the birds of the air and over every living thing that moves upon the earth.' . . . The Lord God took the man and put him in the garden of Eden to till it and keep it" (Gen. 1:28; 2:15). As scholars commonly point out, the first part of this license emerged from a society of herdsmen, while the remainder was the product of a settled agricultural civilization. But what is common to each and most important to both surely consists of the fact that they are descriptions of tasks assigned to a steward.

Think about the New Testment parables having to do with stewards. In the first Christian century, much of Palestine was operated under a system of absentee landlords who owned immense estates, known as latifundia. In this arrangement, the steward was the responsible person while the owner was off somewhere in Italy or Asia Minor tending to other affairs or simply enjoying himself. The steward, with only the broadest directives to guide him, was in complete charge of everything. The principle of latifundia, with God the property owner and humankind his stewards, is just as implicit in God's commandment to "have dominion" over all his living creatures and to "till and keep" his world-sized estate, as it is explicit in those arrangements between God and us human stewards in such familiar New Testament parables as the wicked husbandman (Mark 12:1-11; Matt. 21:33-44), the servant entrusted with supervision (Matt. 24:45-51; Luke 12:42-46), and the talents (Matt. 25:14-30; Luke 19:12-27).

But even in these normative lessons on stewardship, the taint of corruption is already present. The motivation to faithful stewardship is not a desire to serve God for his own sake alone. And worst of all, there is no suggestion that such service is an act of thanksgiving. Rather, the thrust of all these parables concerns what will happen to us if our due stewardship to God is not faithfully rendered. Indeed, the one parable of Jesus that suggests the real reason any Christian ought to be faithful in his or her stewardship to God is a much neglected minor teaching known as the servant's reward (Luke 17:7-10), which ends with this exchange: "Does [the master] thank the servant because he did what was commanded? So you also, when you have done all that is commanded you, say, 'We are unworthy servants; we have only done what was our duty.' "

Thus both the first principle of Christian stewardship—unalloyed devotion to God—as well as its antithesis, already virulently present in Jesus' lifetime, remain major influences upon our proper Christian service today. Paul encountered the same problems in his churches. He even found it necessary to promote stewardship among the Corinthians through such blantant appeals to self-interest as "He who sows bountifully will also reap bountifully"; "God loves a cheerful giver"; and "You will be enriched in every way for great generosity" (II Cor. 9:6-7, 11). Needless to say, budget committees and preachers, in their every-member canvasses and stewardship sermons, continue to stress these same self-serving themes.

But this is a great mistake. God cannot be legitimately served either out of fear or in hope of personal gain. True Christian stewards serve God right where they find themselves, out of hearts overflowing with thanksgiving for all his goodness to them, and out of a clear understanding that they are obliged by their servant status to invest all time, talent, and treasure provided them on his behalf.

We have already mentioned the parable of the talents (Matt. 25:14-30; Luke 19:12-27). Here stands the last word on this subject. An absentee landlord provides each of three stewards with a different sum of money, directs them to invest it for his profit, and goes away on a trip. Upon his return, the landlord calls for an accounting. Two of the servants return the principal together with a profit. The third returns only the original sum, which he had buried in the ground. Now the landlord, who had given each steward a charge commensurate with the individual's ability, gave the two faithful stewards exactly the same reward, even though the size of their responsibilities had varied greatly. But the third steward, who did nothing with the talent entrusted to his care, was promptly discharged from his stewardship. So, Jesus says, God will deal with you and me, judging not on the size of the return, but rather on how faithfully we exercise our stewardship over what he entrusts to our care and keeping.

The antithesis of this viewpoint has always been Christian stewardship "in general," a system admirably designed to encourage personal irresponsibility and the view that Jesus was only joking when he said "every one to whom much is given, of him will much be required" (Luke 12:48). This outlook on the subject, a perception widely held by the more fortunate and prosperous, encourages one to think of a "respectable pledge" or one's "fair share." For the wrong reason, although the problem is real, such individuals also regularly remind any who will listen of the long-term dangers of a few wealthy people underwriting most of any parish church's annual budget.

Another primary encouragement to stewardship "in general" is the United-Way approach to raising the various local, state, national, and international budgets required to conduct the Christian mission of the American church.

Any Christian over forty remembers the days when each parish had its personal missionary whom the congregation directly supported, at least in part. Those were years when most of the things parish churches did in Christian mission were sharply defined, had faces, and were regularly heard from. Nevertheless, assuming a reasonable case is made where the average American Christian can see or hear it, even the more remote elements of the Christian mission have little to fear. All responsible surveys of Christian opinion conducted over the last quarter century indicate that the parish churches of America feel the need for, and are willing to support, denominational hierarchies as well as homeland and overseas Christian missions. Indeed, the idea that the costs of state and national denominational programs must be submerged in something as nebulous as a budget for "our Christian world mission" is one of the principal reasons Christian stewardship in general continues to flourish and Christian mission budgets, in particular, are often so hard to raise.

Christian stewardship gains the attention and respect it deserves only when the enterprise is viewed as a personal, unavoidable obligation that, when not responsibly discharged, fatally compromises one's Christian condition.

The story of the widow's mite (Luke 21:1-4) immediately comes to mind. Much is made of the relative worth, in God's sight, of the poor widow's two coppers when measured against the bags of money contributed by the rich. No knowledgeable Christian would question that the widow's gift was the greater, because the rich "contributed out of their abundance, but she out of her poverty put in all the living that she had." However, there is another point, and that is the one we usually miss. That widow was no idiot. She knew exactly how little those two coppers would mean to the annual budget of the temple. She also knew the snickers her gift would elicit from the busybodies who always hung around those great collection chests to see and report to the neighbors who was giving and how much. Nevertheless, this widow went just to drop two coppers, worth no more than a penny, into the temple treasury. Why did she do it? There can be only one reason. She went because she felt a personal, unavoidable obligation to serve God with what he had entrusted to her. To neglect this obligation would have compromised, if not terminated, her position as his steward. Those rich people who put in the big money flunked as stewards, not so much because they had contributed only "out of their abundance" but even more because of their failure to feel sufficient thanksgiving to God for past goodness to them—expressed as a personal, unavoidable obligation to be stewards of all they possessed, in service to his "kingdom and his righteousness" on earth (Matt. 6:33).

Technique for Christian Stewardship

The place to begin a Christian stewardship program, in any parish church, is with a commitment to full disclosure of all the congregation's financial affairs. Few clergy and boards of trustees have failed to keep their congregations completely informed about the effects of inflation and rising costs on the church budget. But not so very long ago, there was a widespread feeling among those in parish church leadership positions that telling the congregation about all the endowment funds and reserves would hurt the annual pledge drive.

In my experience with three large parish churches, just the reverse has been the case. Before full disclosure was initiated, droves of parishioners had concluded that there was a large quantity of money stashed away in hidden bank accounts and that subsequently there was no need for them to take the annual financial campaign seriously. After full disclosure, each of the three parishes began breaking all previous stewardship records.

Responsible financial management of existing budgets follows close behind. People are not likely to increase contributions to budgets that are badly devised or improperly managed. Many parish church budgets are both. Therefore, one of the most critical steps any parish church can take toward improving next year's every-member-canvass performance involves responsible management of the monies in this year's budget. Keeping the congregation fully informed of the parish's current financial transactions and status is also imperative. Seeking competitive bids on all parish supplies and services likewise builds credibility and usually results in significant savings. Insisting that departmental and program budgets, as established by the annual meeting, be honored is another essential ingredient of fiscal credibility. Overruns should be officially approved by the congregation's senior administrative body. A double-signature voucher system, utilizing purchase vouchers signed by the senior minister as well as the requesting staff member or board, further expands both the image and substance of good money management. And finally, at the end of each fiscal year, the church's books should be formally closed and submitted to an independent audit. Larger churches often have the audit done by a local accounting firm. Three qualified church members, with financial or legal expertise and no official connection to any current boards or committees, will serve just as well. Needless to say, the audit report should be published to the congregation.

Now for the budget itself. A responsible annual budget-setting process is an absolute necessity. However devised, it must be broadly participatory, involving input from all boards and committees. The various institutional structures of the congregation should be requested to submit their budgets for the coming year, given a chance to explain and defend their requests, and then be informed of the actual figures that will afterward be submitted to the congregation for action.

Functional budgeting ought to be mandatory. This is to say that no board or committee should be allowed to submit a general request in round numbers for the wherewithal to fund programs and ministries it has not yet fully worked out. The finance or every-member-canvass committee can perform a service to the entire congregation by precipitating serious reflection upon parish goals, priorities, and the specifics of programs, and by insisting that only completely spelled-out budgets come before it.

Functional budgeting, besides eliminating waste and stimulating program planning, is singularly effective as a means to implementing what emerged from the parish goal-setting process described in chapter 2. A glance at the completed proposal tells any member of the parish whether the next year's church budget represents a valid effort to implement goals, as proposed by the long-range planning committee and adopted by the congregation. Knowing that such a scrutiny will occur, first by the finance or every-member-canvass committee and later by the entire congregation, usually guarantees that parish church boards and committees will submit budgets only for specific programs and needs they have worked out and are prepared to defend.

When the annual budget is completely worked up, it should be published in full to the congregation. This is best done at the beginning of the every-member-canvass effort and in a form most likely to attract the widest possible readership by members of the congregation. It is an excellent idea, after the annual budget has been published and before canvassing actually begins, to offer the congregation an opportunity to ask questions or offer reactions at an open meeting of the entire fellowship. A brief meeting, held immediately following morning worship on Stewardship Sunday, in the sanctuary of the parish church, is a powerfully effective method of accomplishing this with a minimum of effort.

But long before Stewardship Sunday, in fact at least six

months before that date, a finance or every-member-canvass committee needs to begin work on the campaign itself. The ways of going about this are legion. But the causes of poor campaigns are few and strikingly similar. The most common is failure to start working on the campaign soon enough. The most disastrous are relying solely on letters, trusting the Holy Spirit alone, or having no campaign at all.

The first task of the finance or every-member-canvass committee is to lay out its own schedule of exactly when, or by what date, certain things will be done. This calendar thereafter must be adhered to strictly. Then, in consultation with the entire parish church leadership team, an every-member-canvass theme should be selected for the coming year. Media for promoting the drive can then be studied and chosen. Shall we use letters, the church bulletin, displays, brief messages in morning worship? And of these, how many of each or what and when? A pledging apparatus also needs to be devised. This will include designing the pledge cards, settling on the dates when the Stewardship Sunday sermon will be preached, determining when the canvassers and follow-up effort will be put in motion, and deciding when the annual pledges will be dedicated. As part of this process, some means of constantly keeping the congregation informed of where the drive is, over the two- or three-week period it is in operation, should be designed. Of crucial importance is the recruiting of a body of canvassers to make necessary home calls and do the follow-up work.

For the last few years, we have delivered the Stewardship Sunday sermon two weeks before Thanksgiving Sunday, mailed out pledge cards and information to all parishioners the following week, and told them that only those we have not received pledge cards from by a certain date will receive home calls from the canvassers. We always dedicate the parish's annual tithes and offerings on Thanksgiving Sunday. This procedure has allowed us to recruit and train a much smaller group of canvass workers who have real aptitude for such work. About 65 percent of the pledge cards come in without a home call.

There must also be some formal means by which the results

of the campaign can be fully reported to the congregation as soon as possible after the canvass is completed. And no one should ever fear reporting the failures either.

In the midst of a major building program, and with all of Michigan's automobile plants out on strike, we recently undershot our every-member-canvass goal by four thousand dollars. It had been an excellent campaign. Even in that terrible economy, we had surpassed the previous year's pledge income. But still we had not secured enough money to underwrite our very ambitious budget. Being informed of the shortfall, our church council promptly called a meeting of the congregation after church and asked for advice. A motion to extend the campaign for one week, "for the purpose of permitting the congregation to reconsider its pledges" was made and unanimously passed. The following Sunday, the annual budget was over the top, as the result of seventy-two revised pledges that yielded an additional sixty-seven hundred dollars.

Finally, good stewardship technique requires a proper bookkeeping system, an efficient bookkeeper, a responsible group of collectors (who together with the bookkeeper should be bonded), an effective system of monthly or quarterly "friendly reminders" to keep all parishioners current on the state of their pledges, and a monthly report delivered, in published form, usually to the board of trustees, as to the "month" and "year to date" status of the church's receipts and disbursements.

It may seem that what has been set forth under Christian stewardship principles and Christian stewardship technique are two quite dissimilar things. But appearances are deceiving. A modern parish church, in one of its essential aspects, is a nonprofit corporation, which must be operated as a small business. However, the means and ends by and for which that institution operates are those neither of professional fund raisers nor of Wall Street. Indeed, the success or failure of stewardship in any parish church, as well as the outcome of its annual every-member canvasses, will ultimately depend on the congregation's valuation of the church's parochial program and Christian mission. If these are regarded as religiously significant by the majority of the church members, stewardship will prosper. If not, even the most sophisticated and enthusiastic every-member canvass is not likely to reach its goal. Therefore in all undertakings connected with the annual every-member canvass, that parish church will be most successful which remembers best that Christian stewardship is a service rendered solely on behalf of God, out of hearts overflowing with thanksgiving, and with minds directed to rendering the finest possible accounting of time, talent, and treasure, in support of his "kingdom and its righteousness" on earth.

Principles of Christian Evangelism

Evangelism has, for a long time, been a bad word in many parish churches. Well before the American Revolution, it connoted a kind of religious enthusiasm that polite society deemed intrusive and even un-American. Somewhat later, the Constitution of the United States of America confirmed these attitudes. Faced with immense religious diversity, no possibility of a state religion, and a naïve confidence that, given complete freedom of choice, most Americans would choose to be religious, our founders launched us on what Thomas Jefferson called a "fair experiment."[1] The First Amendment to our federal charter set forth its principal conditions in these familiar words: "Congress shall make no law respecting an establishment of religion or prohibiting the free exercise thereof." All of which was soon understood to mean that any American's religion or the lack of it was his or her own private business, and attempting to persuade anyone else on matters of faith just would not do.

So matters stood until quite recently, although it had been noticeable, at least from the end of World War II, that those churches which stressed evangelism were growing faster than those which did not. Then in the mid-1960s, liberal Protestant denominations began to experience a precipitous membership decline. Over the following decade, losses of between 30 percent and 50 percent in stated membership were not unusual. There was a variety of reasons for this decline in active church members, many of which were in no sense a result of evangelism or the lack of it. Nevertheless, the heirarchies of all American communions have recently been reexamining the entire history and method of proclaiming the good news to the unchurched and the uninterested. What they have essentially rediscovered are the original apostolic norms under which the gospel of Jesus Christ went forth from Palestine, even to the "end of the earth." Three of these will be considered in the following discussion.

In the first place, the Christian church has a clear call to unremitting evangelism from her risen Lord.

So we read in the last two verses of the Gospel According to Matthew:

> Go therefore and make disciples of all nations, baptizing them in the name of the Father and of the Son and of the Holy Spirit, teaching them to observe all that I have commanded you; and lo, I am with you always, to the close of the age." (Matt. 28:19-20)

Exactly the same calling of his church into Christian evangelism, though the occasions are less familiar, was reiterated by the resurrected Christ on the road to Emmaus, when he informed Cleopas and a friend: "Thus it is written, . . . that repentance and forgiveness of sins should be preached in [Christ's] name to all nations" (Luke 24:46-47), and just before his final ascension into heaven, when he again declared, this time to all his disciples: "You shall be my witnesses in Jerusalem and in all Judea and Samaria and to the end of the earth" (Acts 1:8).

The viability of the Christian church, nothing less, depends upon what is made of these texts. It is not Jesus of Nazareth's resurrection that makes the difference. The church's one foundation is her faith that Jesus Christ was resurrected Lord! And wherever this be confessed, any bonafide Christian, liberal or conservative, ancient or modern, has no alternative but to discharge the most serious commission this same living, reigning Lord laid on all of us—that of being an evangelist, his proclaimer of the Christian gospel—the good news—"even to the end of the earth."

But a long and often miserable tale began with this commandment. World history is filled with accounts of Christians and Christian churches that have used torture, the stake, imperial armies, and even genocide in futile efforts to "make disciples of all nations." Opponents of Christian evangelism never tire of recalling these dismal happenings, even though such evangelistic practices are completely at odds with all Jesus ever said or did.

Our Lord's intentions are unambiguously set forth in the New Testament. The church is commanded to offer the gospel of Jesus Christ through preaching and teaching, but never to impose it. God and his Christ will make what they will, when they will, out of our poor efforts to be evangelists. Therefore, no parish church need worry about the outcome. The local congregation's sole responsibility consists of making sure that, by all means and in every possible way, it is proclaiming the evangel, the good news of God in Jesus Christ. Indeed, any parish church that is not doing that, no matter what else it may be doing in Christian mission, is not fulfilling its major responsibility as a Christian community.

In the second place, no parish church keeps the second half of the Great Commandment, "love your neighbor as yourself," that does not consciously, constantly, and collectively endeavor to share its Lord with any who have not yet found him.

The ancient American platitude about religion being one's own business rings particularly hollow here. Christ and his good news are not restrictors or diminishers of human life. Rather they constitute the richest gifts any Christian church has to offer to persons who have not yet found them. How then can one love an unchurched neighbor if, through a silly, misplaced concern not to intrude upon his or her privacy, we deny that individual a living Lord and the gospel of Jesus Christ? Or, to make the same point another way, every time a municipal, state, or national election comes around, the great majority of Christian Americans (and especially liberal Protestants) spend hours each day in expressing their personal views on the candidates in an effort to influence the votes of anyone who will listen. But if what we celebrate every Sunday morning in church be true, how does it happen that so few of these same people (and again especially liberal Protestants) are willing to state their personal views on the principal candidate, our Lord Jesus Christ, in the biggest election of all?

One day when Peter and John were going to pray, a lame beggar, seated by the gate of the temple called Beautiful, called to them for alms. Peter turned to him and, there and then, gave that poor unbelieving soul the finest gift any Christian can give a neighbor in need. "I have no silver and gold, but I give you what I have," the apostle declared. "In the name of Jesus Christ of Nazareth, walk" (Acts 3:3).

The call to Christian evangelism involves doing just this. It is the Lord Jesus Christ, his gospel, and God's work of salvation we offer. The miraculous walking of the lame, the seeing of the blind, and the hearing of the deaf are only "outward and visible signs of an inward and spiritual grace" that already moves in the souls of those who accept the good news of Jesus Christ. Indeed, these are exactly the conditions described by the current "born-again Christians." But as the apostle writes: "How are men to call upon him in whom they have not believed? And how are they to believe in him of whom they have never heard? And how are they to hear without a preacher?" (Rom. 10:14). Whatever else it may do by way of "loving the neighbor," a parish church has not even begun to fulfill this obligation until and unless it has made certain that all its lost, wandering, and religiously disadvantaged neighbors have heard the good news of God in Jesus Christ.

In the third place, there is no such thing as a solitary Christian.

By definition, a solitary Christian is both a theological and a practical impossibility. Hence, any parish church that is adequately meeting its obligation for Christian evangelism must be constantly engaged in assisting inactive and unchurched Christians to assume active membership in a local church.

American church membership rolls are scandals. Every sort of inactive, uninterested, no longer resident person can be found registered on most of them. Some few years ago, most denominations made strenuous efforts to encourage roll cleaning. But that work has hardly begun, and unless attitudes about the importance of appearances change, most of it never will be. The fact is that a considerable number of local church clergy and leaders think a large number of names on the church rolls is essential to the parish's local image. Unfortunately, many denominations have further encouraged fictitious membership figures, either through required annual reports or through the tacit assumption that ministers who show significant membership increases will thereby advance their professional careers.

Concern over career advancement led one minister of my acquaintance to confirm children as young as third graders, another to feed fifty or sixty inactives back into the active church member rolls each year of his pastorate, and still another to shelve his own board of deacons' request that the parish secretary promptly inform a church of that denomination in the new place of residence of any church member who moved to another area.

What is overlooked in all this playing at numbers is the immense wastage of Christians that thereby takes place. Mishandling of inactives is where the real damage gets done. These no longer resident or uninterested Christians are just the individuals no one ever calls on or corresponds with, to see if they might not be reactivated as participating members of some Christian congregation.

Paul, in his First Epistle to the Thessalonians, gives us a glimpse of the inactive member problem in the earliest Christian churches, and also some excellent advice as to what we ought to be doing about it. The apostle writes: "Encourage one another and build one another up, just as you are doing. . . . We exhort you, brethren, admonish the idle, encourage the fainthearted, help the weak, be patient with them all" (I Thess. 5:11, 14).

As far as unchurched Christians are concerned, the need for Christian evangelism at the local church level is just as imperative. To this point, when those unchurched Americans who, according to the Gallup poll, regard themselves as Christians, are compared with the number of church members the various communions of the American church collectively claim, an awesome discrepancy appears.

Today, literally millions of Americans apparently believe themselves to be Christians who, though possibly baptized and even confirmed long ago, have not maintained a meaningful relationship with any local congregation in years. Indeed, it may be the greatest Christian tragedy of our times that, because of the reluctance of so many serious Christians to act as evangelists among their unchurched neighbors, the American church has been virtually powerless to do anything about relieving the misery, despair, and hopelessness of so many of this nation's unhappiest citizens.

Something happened on a warm June afternoon last summer that bears repeating here. While working on the outline of this chapter, I broke away to make house calls on two Christian families who had indicated an interest in affiliating with our church. In both cases, a prominent church family, each containing at least one member of our parish leadership team, lived within the same block as those upon whom I was calling. Though one of the new families had been in their present home six months and the other three, neither of our church families had called upon them—not even to welcome these new arrivals to our city.

After making those two new-member calls, I returned to my parsonage. As I entered the back door, the doorbell at the front was ringing. Upon opening the front door, I found myself in the presence of a neatly dressed layman of about forty. He was smiling and in his hands he held an open book. "Sir," he said; "I belong to the Bible Church over on the next block, and I wondered if you have a minute. I'd like to share a verse of God's Word which always has meant a great deal to me."

Technique for Christian Evangelism

Clean membership rolls are the only firm ground on which to raise a proper parish-church evangelism effort. An audit of the entire membership should be conducted each year. Letters ought subsequently to be addressed to all Christians who have permanently moved out of the local area, encouraging them to affiliate with a parish church in the vicinity where they now reside. Denominational officials also suggest that similar letters, reporting the individual's whereabouts, should be forwarded to parish churches located in the vicinity where the person or family has taken up residence.

Confirmed high school and college graduates constitute a special problem. Many of them are at least temporarily uninterested in any church. Especially in middle- and upper-class urban or suburban areas, the largest number of young adults will settle somewhere other than in their hometown after their education is complete. Therefore, in a very few years, this accumulation of absent, uninterested, noncontributing, nonparticipating young people will compose a very significant percentage of the total parish membership unless there is an annual audit and roll cleaning. Like older members who have relocated, these young people ought also to receive letters urging them to join and become active in some local congregation where they now reside.

But the main advantage of an annual membership audit is the opportunity to pick up quickly on inactive members. The board of deacons and deaconesses, or some other body charged with maintaining the membership, ought to assume responsibility for making friendly visitations to any persons appearing on the membership rolls who have not been active over the year past. These home calls should be made at some time other than during the annual every-member canvass. It is a common complaint among the disaffected that "no one ever comes near me except when the church is after money." Many of those so visited at other seasons will return to regular participation simply because of the interest shown. In some cases, hurt feelings will be discovered and the mistake can be repaired. In still others, transportation is the problem, or a pastoral need will be uncovered that should be promptly reported to the minister.

In all these efforts proceeding from the annual membership audit, the primary motive for evangelism ought to be the Christian welfare of the individuals reached. So long as that is seen clearly, the venture will prosper. However, when these undertakings are set in motion to promote parish survival or the budget, the inherent hypocrisy will soon become apparent, and the effort will fail.

Next, attention should be given to the physical condition of the church properties. Are they attractive? Do they invite people to come in? Is adequate parking available? So many churches fail to do little things that make big differences. Attractive landscaping provides the setting. Several properly located bulletin boards, with ever changing information (at least the weekly sermon title) displayed upon them, will pique the interest of those passing by. Easily accessible doorways, adjacent to safe and convenient parking, are invaluable assets. Then there is the matter of exterior lighting. Not only is adequate nighttime illumination a great aid to building security; it will also beautify the corner of the town or city where the church stands, bring Christian inspiration to all who pass by, and provide some of the best promotional advertising any church can buy.

A few years back, I came across a mammoth downtown Gothic church, in a major American city, whose churchyard was a wasteland of weeds and old tin cans, with no exterior lighting to illuminate its beautiful facade at night. Carved in the unwashed stonework over its main entrance was this inscription: "Enter into His gates with Thanksgiving"—but, sad to say, beneath that ornate rendering of Psalm 100:4 glowered an impregnable wrought-iron gate, secured with a great lock upon which hung a large white sign bearing this commandment: "Keep Out!" Apparently most people did—that church is now permanently closed.

Commercial advertising is another evangelism technique that ought not to be ignored. Theologically conservative churches have long made use of lavish display advertising in local newspapers to announce the appearance of visiting preachers or special music. Theologically liberal churches usually settle for modest block advertising, in which the name and address of the church, and next Sunday's sermon title, are prominently displayed. No doubt, those of us who make only minimal use of newspaper advertising ought to reassess our practice. Extravagant display advertising may expend funds that could be spent on the poor but surely we can make better use of local newspapers in getting our ministry before the general public, especially at high seasons of the church year and when special programs are to be offered.

Long experience has, however, convinced me that, for the money, the best use of promotional funds consists of prominently displaying, in the yellow pages of the local telephone book, the parish church's whereabouts, denomination, hours of service, and ministry. Here, liberal churches are often, if not usually, far better represented than conservative churches. Given the latter's major investments in weekly display advertising, this oversight is curious.

A word ought to be inserted at this point as to the usefulness of maintaining a regular weekly broadcast of the Sunday morning worship service. If authentic Christian evangelism, meaning proclaiming the good news of Jesus Christ, is your parish church's main purpose (and it ought to be) then Christian mission dollars can nowhere be more effectively spent than here.

Our Lord's Day service is on the radio every Sunday morning of the year. A very substantial congregation is invariably present in our sanctuary. But the last professional consumer report we received indicated that our church, every Sunday morning, had a radio congregation four or five times as large as the one that was in church.

On the other hand, if your church's purpose is to enlist new pledge-paying, participating members, it will not get its money's worth out of maintaining a regular Sunday morning broadcast. Radio Christians simply are not that often transformed into pew-sitting Christians. Nevertheless, the vote here is an overwhelming yes for regularly broadcasting the Sunday morning worship service, if that opportunity can be arranged. Not only does a regular Sunday radio broadcast greatly extend the influence of any parish church's proclamation of the gospel, but a host of shut-ins, hospitalized persons, and others necessarily at work are blessed and strengthened through this ministry.

Now let us turn to the parish church's programs, operating

procedures, and opportunities that may be directly related to acquiring new members.

Either the board of deacons and deaconesses, a board of greeters, or both, ought to be on duty at every service of public worship. Certainly they should greet member and stranger alike on the way into God's house, but their most important evangelism opportunities always emerge after the service is over. This is to say, many churchgoers habitually arrive late and are primarily interested in getting into a vacant pew sometime before the processional hymn. But after the benediction, they look about, are delighted to be greeted, and usually are quite prepared to settle down for a leisurely talk. Hence whoever does the greeting for a parish church should merely shake hands and say hello on the way in. But after the recessional hymn, they really ought to go to work.

Persons the greeters do not recognize should be greeted with some such phrase as, "I don't believe I know you. My name is John Smith." If the individual so addressed is already a church member, he or she will not be offended, and a new acquaintance results. If the person is not a church member, the way has been opened for a tour of the church, an introduction to the minister, and an invitation "to come back and worship with us again." The greeter should then submit all pertinent information about the visitor, such as name, address, and personal circumstances, to the church office.

Pew cards are indispensable. We tried using the newer and much recommended congregational registration forms, which are passed down the aisle at the time of the offering or during the announcements for all those at worship to sign. This practice disrupted our service, provided no information we had not secured from our previous experience with pew cards, did not measurably increase communications within the parish, and entailed an immense amount of work. A printed pew card, located in a special holder next to the hymn rack, with space for name, address, and specific expressions of need or interest, works wonders. Attention should be called to these instruments at some point during the service. They are filled out by those desiring to do so, and are then placed on the offering plate or returned to the church office.

The parish caller enters right here. Ours is a part-time salaried employee, but a volunteer will often work as well. Every Monday morning, she comes to the church office, reviews the pew cards received the previous Sunday, reads the notes left by our board of greeters, and picks up any other inquiries that have come in during the previous week. She then calls all individuals gleaned from these three sources, making appointments to visit them as soon as possible in their homes. The results of her calls are reported to me. We then initiate an ongoing follow-up, utilizing ministers and other appropriate members of the program staff. Present records indicate that three out of every five individuals or families who sign a pew card, indicating interest in our church, eventually join the covenant membership.

A supporting procedure, which we have found extremely useful, has been our ninety-day *Spire* list. The parish caller puts on this list anyone showing interest in our church, noting the date beside the name. The *Spire,* our messenger, is then mailed to that individual every week for a period of ninety days. If interest continues, this service is extended. After three months, if interest has ceased, the individual's name is removed from the special mailing list. In a few cases, removal has elicited an inquiry as to way the *Spire* stopped coming. We then apologize, put the individual back on the ninety-day *Spire* list, and promptly resume our attentions.

But by far the most important institutional element in a parish church's Christian evangelism program is some form of area-wide outreach organization that is capable of making a large number of original contacts with new arrivals and unchurched persons in the parish's prospect area.

Some years ago, the recommended solution was the creation of a Fisherman's Club. This organization, based upon Christ's word to Peter and the disciples—"Follow me, and I will make you fishers of men" (Matt. 4:19)—usually consisted of a small group of handpicked church members, from different parts of the parish's prospect area and of varying backgrounds, who were particularly good at meeting new people. A more modern and infinitely more effective model, based on similar principles, is a good neighbor program. This organization involves a great many more individuals. Strong church members are enlisted in every part of the parish's prospect area. Each member is assigned three or four streets immediatey adjacent to his or her residence, over which to watch for potential new members. A training session to prepare them for their duties aims at pointing out that every Christian ought to be a good neighbor, being obligated by Christ's Great Commandment to "love your neighbor as yourself." This, at the very least, should result in a "welcome to our neighborhood" visit as soon as practicable after the moving van leaves. Arm twisting is out. The secret of success is being interested in your new neighbor's welfare. If that is really what moves in the heart of the good neighbor when he or she pushes the doorbell, the rest will take care of itself. Homeless Protestants soon reveal their circumstances to sincere good neighbors. An invitation to next Sunday's church service naturally follows. Should the new arrivals be committed members of another religion, sect, or denomination, the good neighbor ought then to make certain this information is immediately passed on to the religious community indicated.

An effective good neighbor program may be organized in pyramid form, with captains for each ten or twelve good neighbors and an overall chairman to whom the captains report each month. Constant reminders and encourgement are required to keep this structure productively active; and, in my experience, sufficient salaried staff support (be it from the parish caller or a minister specifically assigned to this undertaking) is a must.

The chief advantages of the good neighbor program over the fisherman-club approach are the much wider coverage possible since many more parishioners are involved, and the immense value, both in the long and short term, of outreach evangelism's being conducted by someone who will continue to be, even after a prospect has joined the church, his or her Christian good neighbor.

But recruiting new members is of little value unless the parish church keeps them. Those enlisted must therefore be properly prepared for church membership and then adequately supported as they continue in it. A thorough course of new-member preparation, followed by formal reception as members at Sunday worship, fulfills the first need. Some ongoing church body ought to have responsibility for the second. Many churches expect their board of deacons and deaconesses to remain in touch with new members by making periodic visits and telephone calls to inquire how they are getting along over the succeeding eighteen months to two years. We have a board of human resources, one of the six major bodies in our church oganization, whose principal responsibility is to keep all our members involved, as fully as they desire to be, in whatever aspects of our Christian mission they feel called to accomplish or might be most useful in.

Needless to say, recent new members receive very special attention, including the filling out of an interest, experience, and talent file card (one is maintained for every member of our parish), the posting of individual new member photographs on a special bulletin board where they remain for several months, and the tendering of an invitation and free dinner tickets to the first annual meeting of the church after the date they joined our fellowship.

Much of the foregoing, many parish churches have always done. Many procedures are applicable only in particular circumstances. Some of the techniques described and rejected have proved valuable to other evangelism efforts in different parishes. But be this as it may, Christian evangelism, proclaiming the good news of Jesus Christ "even to the end of the earth," remains the parish church's principal responsibility to the kingdom of heaven, God, and his Christ. It is imperative that more of the American church, particularly its liberal parts, begin to treat far more seriously than they traditionally have this inescapable commission. As their still declining membership figures indicate, those that cannot, do not, or will not, shall not much longer continue as significant expressions of American Christianity.

Ministerial Mores and Family Life

What exactly is a Christian minister? You will not find out from the New Testament. The list of ministerial offices supplied by Paul, in his First Epistle to the Corinthians, includes "first apostles, second prophets, third teachers, then workers of miracles, then healers, helpers, administrators, speakers in various kinds of tongues" (I Cor. 12:27). The First Epistle to Timothy and the Epistle to Titus know nothing of these, but rather speak of deacons, elders (presbyters), and bishops (I Tim. 3 and Tit. 1).

The latter configuration probably describes a late first-century, if not a postapostolic, ordering of the clergy. But one thing is certain. You cannot get these two lists of ministerial offices into any coordinated system that might supply the definition of a Christian minister. Actually, until the fourth century, the clerical situation remained extremely fluid. All of which suggests that one needs to look elsewhere for a proper definition of a Christian minister—and specifically of a Christian parish minister.

I would propose that we begin with the word *parson.* This marvelous sobriquet was derived from the far more prosaic word *person,* and the sense of its application is that a parish minister ought to be, in every sense, a representative Christian person.

But what do we mean by a representative Christian person?

Not so very long ago, the parish minister was safely encased in a universal stereotype. He always was a male, wore dark suits, black shoes, and a conservative tie. He didn't smoke, drink, play cards, take his wife dancing, or go to the movies. All members of his immediate family labored under the same kinds of restraints. Some of the parson's next of kin, particularly his children, never recovered from eighteen years on Main Street, right next door to father's church, in a standard-brand American Protestant parsonage.

The new shape of ministerial mores, at least from the standpoint of family life, is incomparably better. In most cases, the parsonage is no longer located next door to the church. The minister and his family dress just like anyone else. The children are free to be like their peers and can play football, ice hockey, or anything else they want.

But this new freedom carries with it new risks. The black suit and the pious whine have been removed. The real parson is now right out front for everyone to see. And for better or worse, the parish minister is going to make it, or not make it, on what he or she as a person actually is.

So we have come full circle. The parson, that representative Christian person, after several centuries of stultifying restraints, is again free to be. And there may be nothing more important he or she can contribute to this morally mixed-up, sexually sick, purposeless generation than a confident, committed image of exactly what any representative Christian person ought to look like.

That is a terribly big order. No minister is equal to the office of parson. But all of us are obliged to try, in the confidence that "God is faithful" and will not let any of his ordained servants "be tempted beyond [their] strength" (I Cor. 10:13). On that head, I remember, as a very young minister who was still quite insecure in his personal faith, coming away from the graveside of a teen-aged boy I had just buried. The father and I walked together to the family car. Neither of us said anything. But just before disappearing inside, the man turned and said: "I don't know if I believe everything you said back there. But it means more than you can imagine for me to know that you believe it." Once more God had proved faithful.

Another poor parson had been brought through duties beyond his strength by powers not his own.

The remainder of this chapter will offer some very personal reflections upon ministerial mores and family life as they apply to the parson's major responsibilities.

Relations with Parishioners

The primary constituency any parson needs to relate to is his or her parishioners. The parish minister has no voice in the matter of who will make up the congregation. They are there—all of them. None can be cast away or avoided. Each must be dealt with, served, and cared for. All of which obliges the parish minister to be extremely sensitive to the way individual parishioners relate themselves to their parson.

In chapter 5, "The Pastoral Care of a Parish," we discussed the difficulties that can be encountered when parishioners seek to exploit their relationship to the parish minister in various unacceptable, offensive, or neurotic ways. Some parishioners, burdened with an unhappy homelife or an impossible boss at work, will vent on the parish minister frustration or anger they dare not express elsewhere. But these crises often represent great opportunities. They present the sensitive pastor, capable of accepting unmerited abuse, with otherwise unavailable openings for the provision of essential pastoral care.

There is a much more mundane, but closely related, matter where pastoral sensitivity must also operate: What's in a name? Some people want to call their minister "Reverend," others "Pastor," and still others "Jim" or "Jane." In each of these instances, a different type of relationship is implied and desired. It behooves any minister to note how the parishioner thus defines their relationship. The only precaution is that the parson must never denigrate his or her office by lowering personal conduct to that which would be unseemly for any seriously Christian person.

I have, after the first act, walked out of plays that offer little more than a lesson in contemporary profanity. I have also made the fastest possible exit consistent with good manners from various parishioners' Christmas parties, wedding receptions, and other high occasions when, as the saying goes, "the party got rough." But here we are on a two-way street. Parish ministers can be grossly insensitive as well. Some years back, when such costume was in vogue, I can recall a funeral where the presiding clergyman appeared at the service with a pair of brown cowboy boots sticking out from beneath the bottom of his Geneva robe. The children of the deceased, to this day, have never forgotten nor forgiven that clergyman.

Another ministerial rule that cannot be ignored without courting certain catastrophe is the ancient stipulation against the parson playing favorites. Every parishioner needs to understand that he or she is always being treated exactly like every other. The minister's maintaining such a stance will alienate a few. For there are those in every congregation who want an inside relationship with the resident parson. If such a relationship is granted, a great and insoluble problem sooner or later appears. No parish minister can retain his or her general effectiveness if a widespread belief exists that the parson is more favorably disposed to certain members of the flock than to others.

Honoraria lie at the very heart of this particular issue. Like a growing number of parish ministers, I have always made it my practice never to accept any sort of remuneration for conducting special offices and sacraments of the church. All honoraria offered for conducting funerals go into the parish memorial funds; all honoraria tendered for conducting weddings are returned as a gift to the couple; and all honoraria received for conducting baptisms are placed in the general fund. My practice is known to the parish. Thus no one ever could conclude I "marry and bury for money," or that the parson might do something for a wealthy family that he would not do for a poor one.

The other side of the same coin is an acknowledgement of my own frailty. Twenty-five or fifty or a hundred dollars would considerably ease almost any parish minister's family budget. Therefore, unless the minister decides in advance that he or she will take nothing for individual services to parishioners, it is virtually impossible not to think about a "fifty-dollar funeral" or a "hundred-dollar wedding." This is the bottom-line reason I refuse all honoraria. Knowing I will reap no personal gain from services to individuals frees me to treat each parishioner exactly like every other, and to devote my full attention to providing them all with the best Christian service within my power.

The most difficult aspect of any parson's relationship with his or her parishioners is deciding what to do when forced to choose between opposing groups within the congregation where a volatile political or social issue is concerned. There are no good answers here. Honorable people have always differred violently over every sort of public issue; and, especially over the last quarter century, the bonds of Christian love (I John 4:7-21) have all too frequently proved inadequate to counteract polarization within a congregation or to spare even the most fair-minded parson.

Every experienced parish minister knows that very few free pulpits exist in the American church today. In chapter 33, "The Public Worship of God," I wrote that the planned Palm Sunday service in 1968 was scrapped at the last moment and replaced by a memorial service for the just assassinated Martin Luther King. That memorial service cost my parish three families. Since then, I have taken other public positions of conscience on extremely serious issues that affected the welare of the entire community. However, I did not employ the pulpit. I have always communicated my position on issues that sharply and bitterly divided my congregation through a signed statement published in the parish messenger. This practice prevents later extravagant expansions upon "what the parson said in his sermon." It also preserves, for everyone, the caring, pastoral, conscience-quickening qualities of the Sunday morning worship service.

But be warned. Even with these precautions, your actions will be misconstrued and your motives impugned. Being right, which cannot be repented, will prove much more of a long-range disaster to relationships than being wrong, which can. It may be true that "pride goes before destruction, and a haughty spirit before a fall" (Prov. 16:18); but, at least over the duration of most pastorates, such justice does not work out in any helpful way between parishioners and parsons. In sum, taking a forthright stand on an issue of conscience is neither forgotten nor forgiven, much less admired, by the majority of parishioners who disagreed with it.

Nevertheless, as each of the foregoing chapters has endeavored to demonstrate, the kingdom of God and its righteousness come first. Therefore, if the parson feels compelled by Christian conscience to speak out on a controversial public issue, then the only right course is to do it! Never be frivolous. Count the cost before entering the battle (Luke 14:28-32). But always remember, the one who leads us laid out the highway to heaven through Gethsemane and Golgotha.

Relations with Neighboring Ministers

Relations between neighboring clergy are seldom as irenic as most of the world imagines. Like it or not, American parish ministers are in competition with one another over everything from new members and community status to the next pastorate.

Separation of church and state, as mandated by the U.S. Constitution, has made membership in a parish church completely voluntary. A very large percentage of American Protestants do not feel a strong sense of denominational identity. Therefore, the fact that a family was Prebyterian, Baptist, or United Church of Christ in one community in no way guarantees they will affiliate with a congregation of the same denomination in the next. The average American family still resides in one place for only five years. These circumstances inevitably mean that, when a new Protestant family moves into an area, every Protestant parish church serving that neighborhood hopes to claim it. Where a particular congregation is regularly more successful than its neighbors in what a clerical friend of mine used to call the new-member sweepstakes, jealously, invidious comparisons, and other sorts of ecclesiastical estrangement often occur. When some local congregation enjoys conspicuous growth over an extended period of time and during a single pastorate, these circumstances can lead to criticism of neighboring local ministers by their own congregations, and will certainly project the senior minister of the high performance congregation into an impossible situation with local clergy—as well as, sooner or later, into much more prestigious employment.

But ministers do not really want to feel this way about one another. It is only partially our fault whenever we do. Indeed, there is significant evidence to suggest that we parsons have always been faced with the need to exhibit an unrealistic kind of loving-kindness to our professional peers that is more than can rightfully be expected. Jesus had his troubles with John the Baptist (Matt. 11:2-6). Paul found himself in contest with Apollos, Cephas, and even his Lord for the loyalty of constituents (I Cor. 1:10-15). Therefore, no one ought to feel unbearably guilty when tempted by jealousy or hostility directed toward a neighboring pastor. The right course is, first, to acknowledge why you feel that way and, second, to do something positive about counteracting it.

A major force for good in alleviating ill feeling between neighboring parish ministers is the monthly clergy breakfast or luncheon. Just getting together in the same room, over a meal, can work wonders. Everyone rediscovers that, after all, we are still just human beings; the sore places are soothed by good fellowship; and a multitude of imagined misunderstandings yield to frank conversation. I am persuaded that the local clergy organization does its most important work for Christ's church right here, and that any minister who does not sit down to breakfast or lunch with his or her professional brothers and sisters in Christ at least four times a year ought to set about providing such an opportunity at once.

There are, however, a number of specific dos and don'ts every parish minister owes to all others. They are of enough importance to be enumerated individually and discussed.

1. Never speak ill of any other minister. Make this a rule, and you will never afterward be embarrassed. Allegations that you authored some disparaging remark about a neighboring parson can then be instantly dismissed. But possibly the major sin avoided is that the Christian ministry in

toto will not be diminished by a parson maligning a fellow member of the practicing clergy.

2. Say something complimentary about a nearby minister every chance you get. Both the neighboring parson and you will be thought the better for it. Your gracious observation will sooner or later reach your neighbor's ear, making a good relationship better or possibly even turning a bad situation into a beautiful friendship.

3. Assist one another whenever possible. If a neighboring minister needs the hospitals covered, a sermon preached, or any other professional office served, do your best to oblige. If he or she gets a good idea for some collective project that will be of real value to the community or the corporate Christian witness, pitch in with a will if asked to join. Do not be one of those entirely too numerous parish ministers who will only work on cooperative Christian efforts they themselves devise and for which they alone expect to get the credit.

4. Never solicit members from a neighboring congregation. Every parish minister is aware that a certain minimal amount of membership mobility occurs among local congregations serving the same area. Even when no invitations or encouragements are extended, it often is impossible to convince the senior minister to whose flock the individual belonged that his or her former parishioner was not enticed away by clandestine activity. The best policy is to require the migrating Christian to do all the work of joining your congregation. I habitually refuse either to get involved or to let any member of my staff become involved with a Christian known to be a member of a neighboring congregation, until that individual has told me directly that he or she desires to affiliate with our congregation.

5. Inform neighboring ministers of situations coming to your attention that may be helpful to them in their ministry. This frequently involves notifying another minister that you have just learned his or her parishioner will enter the hospital for serious surgery tomorrow, but is telling no one. Or it may consist of alerting your colleague to some story running about town that is doing him or her personal harm. Considerable discretion is required here. Even when intentions are of the

best, such information is often ill received. I have been burned as a result of pursuing such good offices more than once. But I would infinitely prefer to suffer a sour-tempered request that I mind my own business than go to bed with information in my possession that might spare a neighboring parson some serious trouble the next day.

6. Do not divulge shared confidences. It has always bewildered me that some parish ministers, who would never think of breaking the pastoral seal where a parishioner's confidences are concerned, will blithely broadcast sensitive or even privileged information gleaned from a fellow cleric. Nothing more quickly destroys good relationships between neighboring clergy than this kind of irresponsibility. On the other hand, few things lead to more genuine or lasting friendships between two ministers than the shared knowledge that neither will ever divulge any conversations between them that are of a confidential nature.

7. Care for one another. The village parson is the only Christian in town without a pastor. Nevertheless, parsons have tragedies, disappointments, illnesses, and deaths with the same frequency as those they serve. But, when the night is darkest, no one calls on the parish minister.

When my father died, two neighboring clergymen did call on me. One was a minister of my own age, with whom I had been at war over several community issues for months. He had lost his own father shortly before, said he knew exactly where I was, and wanted to know if there was anything he could do. We remained on opposite sides of the community issues in question, but from that day on we were friends. The other was an older man. He called at the office the next day and, having expressed his sorrow and desire to help, asked if we might pray. Those two Christian ministers did more for me than they will ever know. For just at the moment when I did not see how the next week's sermon, the pastoral counseling, or another funeral service could be managed, those two marvelous parsons, through simple acts of caring and prayer, enabled me to comprehend with all the saints what is the "breadth and length and height and depth, . . . to know the love of Christ which surpasses knowledge, . . . to be strengthened with might through his Spirit in the inner man" (Eph. 3:18-19, 16).

8. Keep the neighboring clergy on your daily prayer list. Nothing can have a more beneficial effect on the constant competitive stresses existing between neighboring parish church ministers. Unless one has no devotional life at all, it is most difficult to pray every morning by name for those other parsons with whom you share the Christian oversight of a town or city and not begin to care about them as persons. The point here is to get beyond such vague intercessions as the familiar "Almighty and everlasting God; . . . Send down upon our Bishops, and other Clergy, and upon the Congregations committed to their charge, the healthful Spirit of thy grace" into the real "nitty gritty" of praying specifically for the embattled cleric next door, the one who annoyed you last week, or the one whose child is seriously ill in the hospital. Although Christ intends this instruction for the church at large, there is no better strategy for improving relationships with your brother and sister parsons than through spending a part of each day's devotions on individual applications of this familiar portion of the Sermon on the Mount: "Love your enemies and pray for those who persecute you" (Matt. 5:44).

9. Find one or two local parsons with whom you can share the deepest fears, failings, joys, and triumphs of your personal and professional life. The values of a local clergy organization were mentioned earlier. Such gatherings can be wondrously useful in reducing both real and imagined stress brought on by the competitive nature of parish ministry in America. But they will not overcome the loneliness, strengthen the weak knees, or lift the drooping spirits of a parish minister who, while maintaining the necessary presence of confident faith before his or her peers and the world, is nonetheless all dust and ashes inside. Actually, the local clergy association is about the worst place imaginable to vent such fears and feelings. The few times in my experience that a local parson, pushed beyond the breaking point, did unload his burdens at the quarterly ministers' breakfast or luncheon, his peers were of no use whatsoever and, as scripture has it, the last state of that man was worse than the first (Luke 11:26).

Contrariwise, one single parson whose love and caring may be absolutely trusted can return the most discouraged parish minister to that faith which can move mountains. Here is the pastor every parish minister really needs—the Christian who understands exactly where and why it hurts because he or she is also a parson. It takes much time and more knowing to locate the one or two parsons who can fill this office for you. But finding your own personal pastor is worth any effort entailed. The most to be pitied among us are those parish ministers who will not risk that much of themselves in such a relationship with another parson, or those who, imagining themselves self-sufficient, do not believe they will ever need one. While time remains, before the floods come and the winds beat upon your house (Matt. 7:24-27), make sure you have a pastor!

Relations with The Wider Community

Every parish minister, as a representative Christian parson, needs to become and remain productively involved in the wider community. Partially, he or she does so because such activities are worth a portion of any minister's working life. In addition, the parson must set a proper example for his or her congregation and the wider community.

But the primary responsibility is properly serving one's parish church. Therefore, a minister ought carefully to select one or two jobs in the community, and another in some church body beyond the local congregation, with the intention of committing significant personal time and effort to their service. The positions accepted ought to be ones that need attention, are worth holding, and to which the minister feels he or she can make a meaningful contribution. Beyond these carefully selected labors, the parson ought to learn how to say no with a clear conscience and in a gracious manner. A certain few parish ministers who have not mastered the latter tactic or who prefer being out of their parishes to doing the work for which they were called, spend totally unwarranted amounts of time in civic or denominational work. Their own congregations always suffer and, sooner or later, excessive absence discredits their ministry, if it does not cost them their jobs.

The other word that needs to be spoken on this subject concerns the rendering of general pastoral services to unchurched members of the community. Marriages and funerals are often welcomed by clergy who accept honoraria. But there is a wider range of crisis counseling, itinerant ministry, prayers over the city commission, and requested hospitalization visits to unchurched persons that need to be collectively covered by the parish ministers serving a particular area. Simple justice dictates that every parson ought to cover his or her fair share of these time-taxing needs. Since some ministers refuse to do any of these things, those who will usually end up doing more. A moment's recollection of one's ordination vows will, however, convince even the most reluctant that the latter group occupies the only legitimate position any authentic Christian parson ought to accept.

Relations with the Family

Parsonages can be very unhealthy places for spouses (especially wives) and children. There are still congregations who believe that when they hired the minister they employed the rest of the family as well. A slightly larger but often overlapping group of congregations is persuaded that the parsonage itself exists every bit as much for the parish's general use as for the personal pursuits of their minister's family.

But these attitudes, as well as the congregations that hold them, are rapidly disappearing anachronisms. The major problems parish ministers face today in their family relationships are quite commonly of their own devising. They arise from the fact that the minister does not recognize and, if necessary, make clear to the congregation that he or she has a ministry as a family member as well.

Some of the more common forms of this injustice are failure to take a regular day off each week (at a time when the family can enjoy it); taking a church-related vacation (spent, for example, as a staff member at a youth camp) or taking the family to some Christian resort or conference for the family's annual leave (where not only the parson but his or her family will get more of exactly what they live with over the other eleven months of the year); and the kind of ministerial insensitivity that puts speaking to a ladies' guild before celebrating one's wedding anniversary, or sees missing all your son's football games as of less consequence than missing even one meeting of the parish's Golden Age Club. Recently, several of the more far-sighted denominations have been pressing for a policy, in each of their parish churches, of giving ministers one entire weekend off (Friday afternoon through Monday) during each quarter of the church year. This long weekend, not to count as annual vacation, ought to be free of all duties and, if possible, spent entirely away from the parish. From here, that looks like one of the most sensibly helpful ideas to emerge from any denominational office for quite some time.

The thorniest issue pertaining to the parish minister's relationship to his or her family concerns remuneration. Incumbent parsons find it terribly difficult to press for even standard-of-living increments, much less merit raises, without appearing to be more interested in the things of mammon than the things of God (Matt. 6:24). Therefore, what happens automatically on most parishioners' paychecks (and will very soon be complained about or produce a labor union if it does not) often is ignored in the case of the parish minister. Inflation thereafter steadily outstrips salary increments. The parson's family budget falls further and further behind in real spendable income. The only way to recoup what inflation has stolen is to find another church willing to pay more. The parish minister moves, and the whole dreary business starts all over again.

Indeed, this pernicious cycle is the chief reason why, today, one third of the parish clergy in the American church are always seeking a new settlement. But the final irony is that the congregation that failed to keep its parish minister's contract current soon discovers it will have to pay considerably more to hire another, whom they often do not like half as much as the one they lost.

As the years have moved on, I have come to feel somewhat more comfortable about speaking frankly to responsible church officers about the economic realities of staff salaries. Although it was a long time dawning, I gradually awoke to the fact that, by not clearly stating the case for reasonable salaries, I was doing long-term damage to the whole Christian church. Ministers who decide their congregations need to face this issue may find one or more of these arguments helpful:

1. No church can responsibly speak out for social justice that does not pay its own staff a living wage, annually adjusted for inflation.

2. No church has any right to make its own staff bear the cost of its gift to Christian missions by denying its employees deserved salary increments.

3. Parish churches paying unrealistically low ministerial salaries are driving scores of excellent ministers out of the Christian ministry every year, besides diverting an even larger number of potential parish ministers into careers that offer a more reasonable standard of living.

4. Parish churches soon find it impossible to hire or retain quality staff, if salary and fringe benefits do not remain competitive.

When dispassionately offered to open-minded parish leaders (especially those who are currently part of the working force and possess personnel experience), such observations usually produce tolerable economic justice.

But not always. A short while ago, the pastoral committee chairman of one of this country's most substantial Protestant churches informed me that "while we have a fine staff with four excellent ministers, we haven't made the budget in any of the last three years, so naturally we weren't able to give our clergy any salary increases." My wife and I took the first available plane home.

Relations with Oneself

After one has considered all the ways we are related to so many others, the last but most important relationship is the one any parson has with himself or herself. Parish ministry is far too taxing for anyone to undertake who does not love it. As that grand old campaigner Dr. Justin Wroe Nixon used to tell his classes at the Colgate Rochester Divinity School: "If you possibly can bring yourself to do anything else, don't be a parish minister."

Yet unfortunately, because the parish ministry looks like one thing from the outside and something quite different from the inside, a certain number of idealistic young people enter seminary, and then the ordained ministry, under grave misapprehensions about the lifework they have chosen. Some of them weather the storm and emerge in the sunlight of a true vocation. Others, trapped by their training or by unwarranted fears about renouncing their ordination ("No one who puts his hand to the plow and looks back is fit for the kingdom of God"—Luke 9:62), remain unhappy, minimally productive clergy over the balance of their lives. The rest have the good sense to get out.

Respecting the latter option, there are some excellent career assessment centers operated collectively by various denominations. Subsidies are readily available to any minister who, in a mid-career crisis, might benefit from a period of reexamination. These institutions, through testing, professional interviews, and group growth sessions, are usually able to help a minister sort out his or her feelings, assets, and needs, to the end that an intelligent decision, free of guilt and feelings of failure, may be made on the question of remaining in or leaving the professional ministry. It should be mentioned that a variety of excellent, well-paying, highly respected commercial and service institutions are more than happy to hire former parish ministers. To mention a few, insurance companies, newspapers, corporation personnel departments, the administrative and student-service departments of colleges and universities have all found that former parish ministers make superior employees.

The main point is that God does not make mistakes. We do. Therefore, when one of us enters the ordained Christian ministry, only to find out later that he or she does not belong there, God could only hope the person so disposed will have the courage to seek and find the vocation for which he or she was actually created.

What everything comes down to is therefore a calling. Without a call from God into the Christian ministry, parochial life is intolerable. With such a calling, even on the worst of days, any bonafide parson could not imagine being anything else.

And what is a call? Some parish ministers trace their calling to a particular and decisive Damascus road experience (Acts 9:1-19). But the great majority of us gradually grew into our calling only after much doubt, many prayers, and a number of years of observing just exactly what miracles the power of God's Holy Spirit, working through our risen Lord in the midst of a Christian congregation (Matt. 18:20), can produce. The largest number of American parish ministers become reasonably certain they have an authentic calling only after they have spent somewhere between three and five years in active full-time, ordained parish ministry.

The year I graduated from seminary, I was not at all sure the parish ministry was for me. After four years as an apprentice associate, working primarily with young people and on social action, I felt that the parish ministry had become a definite possibility. After five more years, all of them spent as senior minister in an urban church, I knew that I would never want to be anything else but a parish minister. Somewhere in those nine years of sermon manuscripts, baptisms, marriages, night trips to the hospital, funerals, and resurrections, God and his Christ gave me a calling. When it happened I do not know. Where it happened I can not imagine. But that it happened is the thing I am most certain about in my entire life!

I end this chapter and the discussion it concludes with a passage from the writings of the great Charles Haddon Spurgeon (1834–1892) to which, in times of spiritual dryness and discouragement, I have returned again and again. My closing prayer is that these majestic sentences may uplift and encourage a multitude of other very ordinary parish ministers, who daily seek to act the part of authentic Christian parson:

By all the castings down of His servants God is glorified, for they are led to magnify Him when He sets them on their feet, and even while prostrate in the dust their faith yields Him praise. . . . Such mature men as some elderly preachers are, could scarcely have been produced if they had not been emptied from vessel to vessel, and made to see their own emptiness and the vanity of all things around about them. Glory be to God for the furnace, the hammer, and the file. Heaven shall be all the fuller of bliss because we have been filled with anguish here below, and earth shall be better tilled because of our training in the school of adversity.

The lesson of wisdom is be not dismayed by soul-trouble. Count it no strange thing, but a part of ordinary ministerial experience. Should the power of depression be more than ordinary, think not that all is over with your usefulness. Cast not away your confidence, for it hath great recompense of reward. Even if the enemy's foot be on your neck, expect to rise and overthrow him. Cast the burden of the present, along with the sin of the past and the fear of the future, upon the Lord who forsaketh not His saints. Live by the day—aye, by the hour. Put no trust in frames and feelings. Care more for a grain of faith than a ton of excitement. Trust in God alone, and lean not on the needs of human help. Be not surprised when friends fail you: it is a failing world. Never count upon immutability in man: inconstancy you may reckon upon without fear of disappointment. The disciples of Jesus forsook him; be not amazed if your adherents wander away to other teachers; as they were not your all when with you, all is not gone from you with their departure. Serve God with all your might while the candle is burning, and then when it goes out for a season, you will have less to regret. Be content to be nothing, for that is what you are. When your own emptiness is painfully forced upon your consciousness, chide yourself that you ever dreamed of being full, except in the Lord. Set small store by present rewards; be grateful for earnests by the way, but look for the recompensing joy hereafter. Continue with double earnestness to serve your Lord when no visible result is before you. Any simpleton can follow the narrow path in the light: faith's rare wisdom enables us to march on in the dark with infallible accuracy, since she places her hand in that of her Great Guide. Between this and heaven there may be rougher weather yet, but it is all provided for by our covenant Head. In nothing let us be turned aside from the path which the divine call has urged us to pursue. Come fair or come foul, the pulpit is our watch-tower, and the ministry our warfare; be it ours, when we cannot see the face of our God, to trust under the shadow of His wings.[1]

Notes

Chapter 1

1. See Heinrich Greeven in Gerhard Kittel, *Theological Dictionary of the New Testament,* trans. G. W. Bromiley (Grand Rapids: Eerdmans, 1973), II, 803.
2. Forbes Robinson, *Letters to His Friends* (New York: Longmans, Green, 1912), pp. 96-97.
3. George Bernanos, *The Diary of a Country Priest,* trans. Pamela Morris (New York: Macmillan, 1938), pp. 28 ff.

Chapter II

1. (Nashville: Abingdon, 1978.)

Chapter III

1. Gregory Dix, *The Shape of the Liturgy* (London: Dacre Press, 1964), p. 1.
2. John Skoglund, *A Manual of Worship* (Valley Forge, Pa.: Judson Press, 1968), p. 15.
3. (London: Oxford University Press, 1945), p. 5.
4. See *An Order of Worship,* published by the Executive Committee of the Consultation on Church Union (Cincinnati: Forward Movement Press, 1968).
5. (New York: Scribner's, 1934), pp. 287 ff.
6. Paul Scherer, *The Word God Sent* (New York: Harper, 1965), p. xi.

Chapter IV

1. Large churches often operate three youth fellowships, either with the ninth grade isolated between the two lower grades and the three higher grades; or they evenly divide the six junior and senior high school years into three two-year youth fellowships.
2. "The Healthy Personality," in *Psychological Issues,* International Universities Press, Vol. 1, No. 1, p. 92.

Chapter V

1. *The Meaning of Pastoral Care* (New York: Harper, 1966), p. 8.
2. Wayne E. Oates, *Pastoral Counseling* (Philadelphia: Westminster Press, 1974), p. 52.
3. New-member counseling, involving Christians who transfer from other parishes, can serve as another very useful form of instructional pastoral care.
4. (New York: Macmillan, 1969.)

Chapter VI

1. Sidney Mead, *The Lively Experiment* (New York: Harper, 1963), pp. 55 ff.

Chapter VII

1. *Lectures to My Students* (Complete and Unabridged), published in the United States by Zondervan Publishing House by special arrangement with Marshall, Morgan and Scott Ltd. of London, pp. 164-65.